Berlioz's Semi-Operas

Roméo et Juliette and *La damnation de Faust*

Daniel Albright

Ⓡ University of Rochester Press

First published 2001
by the University of Rochester Press

The University of Rochester Press is an imprint of Boydell & Brewer, Inc.
668 Mt. Hope Avenue, Rochester, NY 14620, USA
and of Boydell & Brewer, Ltd.
P.O. Box 9, Woodbridge, Suffolk IP12 3DF, UK

ISBN 1–58046–094–1
ISSN 1071–9989

Library of Congress Cataloging-in-Publication Data

Albright, Daniel, 1945–
  Berlioz's semi-operas : Roméo et Juliette and La damnation de Faust / Daniel
Albright.
    p. cm. — (Eastman studies in music, ISSN 1071-9989 ; vol. 14)
  Includes bibliographical references (p.) and index.
  ISBN 1-58046-094-1 (alk. paper)
  1. Berlioz, Hector, 1803–1869. Roméo et Juliette.   2. Berlioz, Hector, 1803–1869.
Damnation de Faust.   3. Shakespeare, William, 1564–1616. Romeo and Juliet.
  4. Goethe, Johann Wolfgang von, 1749–1832. Faust.   I. Title.   II. Series.

ML410.B5 A63 2001
782.1'092–dc21   21001023767

British Library Cataloguing-in-Publication Data
A catalogue record for this book is
available from the British Library

Designed and typeset by Straight Creek Bookmakers
Printed in the United States of America
This publication is printed on acid-free paper

Contents

Illustrations

Music Examples

All the examples are by Berlioz.

Preface

We usually use the term *semi-opera* to refer of the English opera of the later seventeenth century. Purcell's contemporary Roger North thought that it was wrong to speak of *King Arthur*, or *The Fairy Queen*, or *The Indian Queen* as a true opera, because each contained such large quantities of ordinary spoken drama; he thought it better to call such a work a *semi-opera*, because some scenes were completely spoken, others completely sung, and still others mostly spoken, but including incidental songs.

I feel that *Roméo et Juliette* (1839) and *La damnation de Faust* (1846) together occupy and fill an ecological niche within the full taxonomy of the work of Hector Berlioz (1803–69); and, in casting about for the right genre-term, I light upon *semi-opera,* in a somewhat different sense from North's. Neither includes any speech at all, but each is like a Purcellian semi-opera demoted from stage to concert hall, with all the talking parts left out: a strange mélange of disconnected scenes, in which the gaps are either left gaping, or covered over with obviously ineffectual transitional material—ineffectual, that is, from the standpoint of an actual stage work. Each is an experiment in wresting drama into music, in a format liberated from the conventions and exigencies of stage production. In the old semi-operas, Purcell set those parts of the text that were intended for musical expression, and left the prosaic parts to the skills of actors, not singers; in the two newer semi-operas, Berlioz deleted the prosaic parts, and either set those texts that stimulated his imagination, or wrote orchestral pieces based on such texts.

Berlioz completed three genuine operas, but few of his experiences in the lyric theatre were happy. Many factors were involved here: his fiery and irascible character, which repelled important stage administrators; his work as a music critic; his musical style, not always grateful to the ears of the public; and also his impatience with the rigidity of the genre of opera during his productive lifetime (the mid-1820s through the early 1860s). Berlioz wanted to arrogate to himself certain freedoms that were simply not available to the opera composers of the age, who were at the mercy of singers' demands for stereotyped arias, as well as the public's demands for conventional plots; and so Berlioz devised operas for the private spaces of imagination, spaces where a cello could sing the role of Roméo if desired, spaces in which elaborate operatic scenes could be erected in an instant, then switched off at pleasure.

Both Shakespeare's *Romeo and Juliet* and Goethe's *Faust* were plays that strongly challenged the conventions of drama in nineteenth-century France. It is a familiar tale, how a company of British actors visited France in 1827; how the French were astonished by the Shakespearean theatre, with its reckless admixture of comedy and tragedy, with its bizarre negligence of the rules of unity; how Berlioz fell in love with the actress who played Juliet, Harriet Smithson. A little less familiar is the fact that in 1827 the stages of Paris were full of Faust plays (by Jouy, and Théaulon and Gondelier), including a Faust opera (libretto by Béraud and Merle, music by Louis Alexandre Piccinni)—all following from a French enthusiasm for Goethe's *Faust* that nevertheless had trouble stomaching anything like a close version of Goethe's text.[1] Shakespeare's play was alien because of its antiquity and its dramaturgy—its composition for a stage without a proscenium arch, its spatial and temporal outrages; Goethe's play was alien because of its subordination of all dramatic elements to verbal patterning, its refusal to submit to any of the demands of the theatre (a finite number of scenes; an orderly development of action)—in *Faust* the actors fly, ride on pigs, and so forth. *Faust* is a closet drama, or, more exactly, a drama ideally fitted for intimate theatricals among the cultural élite: Goethe himself liked to play the role of Mephistopheles in productions with his friends.

The French theatre, then, was struggling to find ways of meeting the challenges presented by Shakespeare and Goethe—how could these important but uncomfortable dramaturgies be assimilated into the canons of the stage? Berlioz was willing to go further than anyone else, by dismantling the concept of opera, the concept of theatre itself. To Berlioz, Shakespeare and Goethe seemed to be moving toward a vision of drama as fluid, as biologically potent, as the new discourse of Romantic music; and so he founded a new genre, an internalized music drama of swelling and detumescence, engorgement in fantasy followed by disillusion. By cracking the fixed shell of the nineteenth-century theatre, Berlioz was able to devise a more intimate hybrid between music and drama—a semi-operatic, semi-symphonic thing.

It is impossible to overestimate the importance to music history of the work of Shakespeare and Goethe—especially Shakespeare. The English semi-opera of the seventeenth century developed out of the attempt to find a musical response to Shakespeare's work: John Dryden considered that the first English opera was the 1674 version of *The Tempest,* as revised by Davenant, Shadwell, and Dryden himself, with music by Locke, Humfrey, and Reggio; and Dryden should know, for he was the most distinguished English librettist of the age. Shakespeare looms large over the whole field of semi-operas: Purcell's *The Fairy Queen* (1692–93) is based on *A Midsummer Night's Dream*; and Purcell (or perhaps his pupil John Weldon) composed in 1695 still another version of *The Tempest,* with completely new music. Berlioz's creation of a new musical genre through close attention to Shakespeare only continued a line of development that had begun centuries before. Shakespeare's extraordinary facility in modulating from the highest poetry to the most vulgar prose provided a model for an inclusive music theatre (either actual or virtual), easily moving from the spoken to the operatic.

The method of critical inquiry used in this book is somewhat unusual.

I've tried to give roughly equal weight to the textual model (Shakespeare or Goethe) and to its afterlife in Berlioz; I provide a detailed consideration of the theatrical aesthetic of the writer, followed by a detailed scrutiny of the inner workings of the fantasy-theatre implied by Berlioz's music. Throughout this book I assume that Berlioz *interprets* Shakespeare and Goethe, and provides insights into their work difficult to obtain otherwise. Berlioz was himself an extremely able critic, but his best literary criticism can be found within his music—my task is to re-state in words what Berlioz says through the orchestra and the singers.

Berlioz has been fortunate in his own critics. Distinguished men of letters with extraordinary musical sensitivity, and distinguished musicologists with extraordinary literary sensitivity—Jacques Barzun, Hugh Macdonald, David Cairns, Julian Rushton, and D. Kern Holoman, among others—have together compiled a body of Berlioziana that is one of the glories of musicology. I hesitate to add my voice to this articulate counterpoint of scholarly opinions. But perhaps the chorus can be strengthened by yet another voice, even if it's a soft baritone with a limited range.

This book bears from the beginning a great debt to three of my friends. Professor Ralph Locke—a Berliozian of infinite aplomb and panache—encouraged this project from the beginning, worked with me closely on its first installment (an article on *La damnation de Faust* in the *Journal of Musicological Research,* 1993), and has provided a steady flow of wisdom ever since. For some years, Professor Kenneth Gross—the great expert on noises in Shakespeare—and I have been collaborating on a course on Shakespeare and Music, and the first half of this book stems directly from our conversation, both with each other and with our students. I wince when I consider how much of this book is actually his intellectual property, even those parts that I think are entirely my own. And I thank Su Yin Mak, who is also a teaching collaborator of mine—this time in a course on the semantics of music—as well as my music teacher. She worked with me with amazing resources of patience and good will, and I will always be in her debt.

In later stages of its development, this book had the good luck to be read by Julian Rushton, David B. Levy, and (in part) David Gramit, who were generous enough to correct some errors and to contribute striking insights of their own. And finally a *reverenza* to Jennifer Brown, who pored over this text with good-humored rigor and a sort of stringent mercifulness; an expression of amazement to my editor, Louise Goldberg, who seems to know everything about editing and everything about Berlioz, and who was delightful to work with on this book; and an acknowledgment to my Universal Object of Acknowledgment, Karin.

Note: I claim responsibility for all the translations in this book, unless otherwise indicated in the notes.

Earlier versions of some of the material about *Roméo et Juliette* and about *La damnation de Faust* appeard in my two articles in the *Journal of Musicological Research*: "Berlioz's *Faust*: The Funeral March of a Marionette," *JMR* 13, 1–2 (1993): 79–97; and "Berlioz's *Roméo et Juliette*: Symphonic Metamorphoses on a Theme of Shakespeare," *JMR* 19, 2 (2000): 135–76.

The music examples are taken from the following scores in Berlioz, *New Edition of the Complete Words,* edited by Hugh Macdonald (Kassel, New York: Bärenreiter, 1967–), and are used with permission:

> *La damnation de Faust,* vol. 8, edited by Julian Rushton, and its accompanying vocal score.
> *Villanelle* from *Les nuits d'été,* vol. 13, edited by Ian Kemp.
> *Roméo et Juliette,* vol. 18, edited by D. Kern Holoman, and its accompanying vocal score,
> *Symphonie fantastique,* vol. 16, edited by Nicholas Temperley.

Daniel Albright
Rochester, New York
February, 2001

Berlioz's Semi-Operas

1. Illustration from Charles Sorel's *The Extravagant Shepherd; Or the History of the Shepherd Lysis. An Anti-Romance; Written Originally in French, and Now Made English.* London, Printed by T. Newcomb for Thomas Heath, 1654. Photograph from the Library at the University of Michigan. Used with permission.

I

Shakespeare's *Romeo and Juliet*

1. Introduction

Every opera is a transgression against itself. Music always ends by both reinforcing and contradicting the verbal text that it tries to set; for music is far more rich in interrelations, far more semantically replete than spoken drama. The thrill is always a mixture of the right thrill and the wrong thrill. The best libretti leave a great deal of room for misunderstanding why a character is moved to sing.

Shakespeare's *Romeo and Juliet* looks like the ideal play for an opera, full of all sorts of possibilities for transgression: the rebellion of love against authority, the rebellion of giddy poetry against the common prose of domestic arrangements, the rebellion of spontaneity against prefabricated social structure. But these rebellions are largely illusory: Romeo and Juliet become outlaws in one social system, only to become obedient servants of another social system. *Romeo and Juliet* is a profoundly hemmed-in play, in which every assertion of freedom is in fact a restriction, until finally the space that the lovers can occupy contracts to the size of a vault in a tomb. No completely successful Romantic opera was ever written on this play, partly because Romeo and Juliet, like their parents, are instinctive conformists. Their poetry bears only a superficial resemblance to Romantic poetry; in fact it is written strictly to rule.

Still, the fact that the play's theme is love—love grown huge and intense—has long made it attractive to opera composers. All-compulsive love is a rare premise in Shakespeare's works; this feature of the canon, which tends to make Shakespeare dispiriting to musicians, drew the strong applause of Samuel Johnson in 1763:

Upon every other stage [than Shakespeare's] the universal agent is love, by whose power all good and evil are distributed, and every action quickened or retarded. To bring a lover, a lady and a rival into the fable; to entangle them in contradictory obligations, perplex them with oppositions of interest, and harass them with violence of desires inconsistent with each other; to make them meet in rapture and part in agony; to fill their mouths with hyperbolical joy and outrageous sorrow; to distress them as nothing human ever was distressed; to deliver them as nothing human ever was delivered, is the business of a modern dramatist. For this probability is violated, life is misrepresented, and language is depraved. But love is only one of many passions, and as it has no great influence upon the sum of life, it has little operation in the dramas of a poet, who caught his ideas from the living world, and exhibited only what he saw before him. He knew, that any other passion, as it was regular or exorbitant, was a cause of happiness or calamity.[1]

The elder Capulet could not have expressed the case against love so well.

But the case against love is also the case against opera, for an opera libretto, from Monteverdi's time to ours, has its chief purpose in filling the mouths of the characters with hyperbolical joy and outrageous sorrow, by distressing them as nothing human was ever distressed. Johnson considered opera—he was thinking particularly of opera performed in a language the audience didn't understand—to be an "exotic irrational entertainment"; and he clearly liked a play to the exact extent that it didn't resemble an opera. Johnson was a classicist, with little taste for the flamboyant and sensational; he inherited some of the old Greek or Roman feeling that extreme love was a useless and ignoble condition, preventing a warrior from fighting well, or an honorable man from behaving honorably. (A century before Johnson's time, Racine spoke, in *Phèdre*, of love as a carnivore on the hunt, or a monstrous parasite: *Vénus toute entière à sa proie attachée.*) But was Shakespeare also a classicist in this sense? Did Shakespeare wish to scale down the role of love in human life? *Romeo and Juliet* is a laboratory designed to test this case: is love a curse, or a blessing, or a trivial aspect of human life that sometimes gets out of control? The answer to this question will determine whether *Romeo and Juliet* in some sense wants to be an opera. In an opera, love may be a curse or a blessing; but there are few operas where love is dismissed with a yawn, or a sad shake of the head.

2. The Veronese Social Code

The plot concerns three families and two codes of conduct. Everyone remembers the Capulets and the Montagues, but it is important to remember that there is another family as well, the family that comprises Prince Escalus, Mercutio, and Paris (3.1.145; 5.3.75, 295); we'll see soon that the kinship of these three disparate men is significant. Similarly, everyone remembers that there is a code that governs the behavior of the elders of the play, but it is important to remember that there is another code, the code of Romeo and Juliet, which assaults the first code. The code of the young lovers is subversive, but the protocols of its subversion are wholly formalized and articulate. It is as if there were Ten Commandments for the ordinary folk, and ten more commandments—written in smaller print—for those who chose to disobey the first set of rules. The world of Verona has many possibilities for transgression, but all law-breakers are caught up in some minuet or other, for transgression is itself a dance. First we'll examine the social code, then the code of love.

The tenets of the Veronese social code are many and complicated, regulating everything from table manners to the construction of rituals for marriage and burial; and the code is made still more complicated by the existence of subcodes, since the upper and the lower classes, the young and the old, the clergy and the laity, all live by slightly different rules, within a general field of agreement. The decorum of the older upper classes can be gathered from the speeches and behavior of Capulet and Lady Capulet. They are a pair of ceremonious tribalists, who believe that true intimacy is a direct function of the immediacy of family relation. Here the chief rule is: blood is thicker than water. Honor, therefore, is essentially familial, not personal, and an insult to one Capulet is an insult to all; as Mervyn James puts it, "a man's very being as honourable had been transmitted to him with the blood of his ancestors, themselves honourable men. Honour therefore was not merely an individual possession, but that of a collectivity."[2] The law code of the Capulets (and here it diverges from the code of Prince Escalus) is *vendetta*: offenses are avenged by one's kinsmen, not by jurisprudence. Honor is so exigent that even the old head-of-clan must wield his long sword when a brawl arises (1.1.75). And yet, though the code not only permits street brawling but commands it, the code also observes the punctilio of the rite of *hospitium*: after Romeo is recognized at the Capulets' ball, Capulet refuses to permit his wife's hotheaded nephew Tybalt to assault Romeo (1.5.65)—the household is sacrosanct, and even an uninvited enemy must be treated hospitably. It is all tribal warfare, but conducted (so to speak) under the marquess of Queenberry's rules.

Of course, the same principles govern the conduct of the Montagues. One of the strangest and most significant aspects of Shakespeare's play is the absolute arbitrariness of the feud. Generally warfare in literature exists between parties with distinguishable cultures or values: good versus evil (*The Castle of Perseverance, Paradise Lost*); those touched by God with a mission to conquer, versus the natives (the Israelites and the Canaanites in *Exodus*, Aeneas and Turnus in the *Aeneid*); the intelligible West versus the exotic East (*Antony and Cleopatra, Lakmé*); new competence versus archaic incompetence (*Richard II, Prometheus Unbound*). But Shakespeare was extraordinarily intrigued by the dramatic possibilities of warfare for warfare's sake—between parties who, confronting one another on the battlefield, simply stare into a mirror. The House of Lancaster and the House of York in the *Henry VI* plays are disputants more easily discriminated by the colors of their badges than by culture or by values; and the warring parties in *Romeo and Juliet* are wholly interchangeable—well might Juliet ask, "What's in a name?" (2.2.43), for there is nothing to discriminate Capulet from Montague except the sound of the word. There is no mythology for the source of the feud, as if everyone has long since forgotten why Montagues and Capulets are in a state of discord; it is a pure given. As Arthur Brooke presented the background in Shakespeare's principal source, *The Tragicall Historye of Romeus and Juliet, written first in Italian by Bandell, and now in Englishe* (1562):

> There were two ancient stocks, which Fortune high did place
> Above the rest, indued with wealth, and nobler of their race,
> Loved of the common sort, loved of the prince alike,
> And like unhappy were they both, when Fortune list to strike;
> Whose praise, with equal blast, Fame in her trumpet blew;
> The one was clepéd Capulet, and th' other Montague.
> A wonted use it is, that men of likely sort,
> (I wot not by what fury forced) envy each other's port.
> So these, whose egall state bred envy pale of hue,
> And then, of grudging envy's root, black hate and rancour grew. (ll.
>   25–34)

According to Brooke, the Montagues and Capulets quarrel precisely because there is no other way to tell them apart.

In a culture based on honor, exact equality is the most distressing and untenable of all conditions. Mervyn James notes that

> . . . in the company of his equals a man was expected to assert his "pre-eminence," a requirement which imparted a note of tension even to ordinary social intercourse and daily conversation. So much so that Guazzo [in *The Civile Conversation of M. Steeven Guazzo*, tr. George Pettie, 1581] advised the gentleman to seek relaxation in the company of his inferiors. For with them "he shalbe the chief man . . . and rule the company as his list; neither shall he be forced to favor or do anything contrary to his mind; which libertie is seldom allowed him amongst his equals"; for they "will looke for as much prehemminence every way as himself." . . . the persistent tension meant that violence was always liable to escalate from its latent to an actual state, when its expression was the armed conflict of a duel.[3]

But of course, among exact equals, pre-eminence by definition does not exist; and so two honorable men, trapped in an unhappy state of identicality, will continually seek out, by various useless challenges, some basis for establishing a relative rank. And, if all else fails, exact equals can create a kind of fetish around the one property that always retains a power to discriminate: the name. *Capulet* and *Montague* become charged, explosive terms.

In this way, names become a kind of weapon against the named. The code demands an antagonist, if such concepts as honor, vendetta, hospitium, are to be put in play at all; therefore the code-driven Veronese will sink into a state of utter lethargy unless the play of signifiers can generate an enemy. In a sense this aspect of Shakespeare's thinking is deeply musical, for patterns of musical antithesis are mostly arbitrary—for example, dominant is opposed to tonic only formally, not semantically; but the notion of interchangeable opponents nevertheless runs counter to the instincts of opera composers, who like warring tribes to have the maximum audible distinguishability—as when Sondheim and Bernstein, in *West Side Story,* made one of the rival gangs Puerto Rican. And yet the point of Shakespeare's feud is that Montagues and Capulets dress alike, think alike, talk alike, agree on everything; their dispute is lexical, not cultural. They are enemies because the attribute *noble* (as they understand it) cannot display itself in a condition of peace. A culture predicated on dispute will, sooner rather than later, find a dispute to generate the culture.

This line of argument follows from René Girard, who finds, in his superb book on envy in Shakespeare's plays, that the wellspring of social antagonism is excessive likeness: friends (such as Valentine and Proteus in *The Two Gentlemen of Verona*) tend to imitate one another, and this assimilation is likely to terminate in a state of complete jealousy and hatred:

> Tragic antagonists do not fight about "values"; they desire the same objects and think the same thoughts. . . . Deep in the human psyche, mimetic rivalry reaches the identical essence of concord and discord in human affairs.[4]

In music, the most wrenching dissonances come from intervals that are *almost* unisons; and *Romeo and Juliet* is a study of the extremes of hate and love that arise from the unbearable tension of equality.

In *Romeo and Juliet,* Veronese society has codified envy into a formal rule of behavior, a bad commandment. The play is a study of the essential inadequacy and incoherence of the social code that fosters feuding—indeed the feuding is itself a sign of the code's intrinsically self-destructive character. The contradictoriness of the Veronese social code is most conspicuously exposed by the issue of marriage. Marriage is a matter of difficulty because it brings two of the code's tenets into conflict: the rule of vendetta and the rule of *exogamy.* Marriage cannot take place between a boy and a girl in the same family; but a strange family is always the object of suspicion, if not of outright vendetta. Therefore the family is exposed, pried open, in dangerous ways by any child who seeks to marry; and parents will go to great trouble to ensure that this threat to the integrity of the family is kept as small as possible. The code insists that the love of husband and wife, since it arises from an extrafamilial bond, must be subordinate, inferior to, the love of parent and child—at least until the passage of years so fully assimilates the foreign mate into the family that all foreignness has vanished. According to the code, a parent has the duty to point and fasten his daughter's affection to any object he thinks proper—as if the daughter's affection were simply a limb or tentacle of his own wise and seasoned desire to shape a proper family. When it is time for Juliet to marry, her father's code requires him to treat her with elaborate courtesy—these are not barbarians, but supersubtle Veronese. Capulet tells Paris, the man he's chosen to be Juliet's husband,

> Earth hath swallowed all my hopes but she;
> She's the hopeful lady of my earth.
> But woo her, gentle Paris, get her heart,
> My will to her consent is but a part;
> And she agreed, within her scope of choice
> Lies my consent and fair according voice. (1.2.14–19)[5]

Capulet's good will and devotedness to Juliet are clear; he hopes that the choice of a husband will be a kind of collaborative venture between father and daughter. On the other hand, "her scope of choice" is obviously narrow; and Capulet assumes that an obedient daughter will finally acquiesce in any choice her father makes:

> Sir Paris, I will make a desperate tender
> Of my child's love. I think she will be rul'd
> In all respects by me; nay more, I doubt it not. (3.4.12–15)

When it happens that Capulet's choice and Juliet's diverge overwhelmingly, Capulet tells her that she will marry Paris in St. Peter's Church, "Or I will drag thee on a hurdle thither. / Out, you green-sickness carrion!" (3.5.155–56). The code demands that Capulet treat his chattel with courtesy and esteem, unless she asserts some independence from familial control.

How does the code sort out and evaluate prospective suitors for the hand of the family daughter? Obviously, such factors as wealth and noble title are important, but in fact Juliet's parents assume (perhaps with a canny understanding of the psychology of sheltered thirteen-year-old girls) that these aren't the factors to emphasize in order to increase Paris's glamour in her mind. Instead Lady Capulet stresses his good looks:

> Read o'er the volume of young Paris' face,
> And find delight writ there with beauty's pen;
> Examine every married lineament,
> And see how one another lends content;
> And what obscur'd in this fair volume lies
> Find written in the margent of his eyes.

This precious book of love, this unbound lover,
To beautify him, only lacks a cover. (1.3.81–88)

Lady Capulet seems chiefly concerned with the aesthetics, perhaps the eugenics, of the match: she wants for Juliet an ornamental husband, a prettily figured text, to be made still more handsome by Juliet's hand-rubbed soft binding. Lady Capulet's language is veiled, metaphorical, even lascivious, as if she were subverting Juliet's own language in order to put thoughts into Juliet's head. The rhymed couplets don't fall into the pattern of a sonnet, but there is a world of love poetry behind Lady Capulet's speech: it is not far from her "Examine every married lineament, / And see how one another lends content" to "Mark how each string, sweet husband to another, / Strikes each in each by mutual ordering" (Sonnet 8). But Lady Capulet's speech is an affair of advertising, not an affair of literature: she's only trying to cast an erotic halo around Paris for pragmatic reasons. For Lady Capulet, suitors tend to be interchangeable, except insofar as such factors as wealth and clan and beauty can provide means of differentiation; she isn't concerned with the metaphysics of kissing. At the end of her speech, the Nurse interrupts with a pregnancy joke—exactly as Mercutio interrupts Romeo's high-flown rhetoric with coarse puns. But Lady Capulet is herself a sort of ironist: when she tells Juliet that Paris "only lacks a cover," she in effect cues the audience's own inner Nurse or Mercutio to supply a line about women who cover men by lying on top of them.

The social code assumes that love is sensible, that it is an amorphous sensation of pleasure that might fasten itself to a great many different objects, but will finally fasten itself to the most socially advantageous suitor. From the code's point of view, human beings are texts to be organized into the Dewey Decimal System of social life: Juliet, like Paris, is a book, onto whose pages paragraphs of propriety, quoted from the code itself, are to be inscribed. But, as we'll see, some of Juliet's pages are printed with shocking words, words rarely to be found in manuals of conduct for young girls.

This is not to say that Veronese social code is oblivious to sex: all matters pertaining to sex tend to trouble the code, to summon its exercise of power. The code has the strength to domesticate and formalize human sexuality, even among horny adolescents. The code clearly acknowledges that love is more than prudence, more than mutual respect, more than aesthetics: it's also erotic. For the elderly Capulets, this aspect of love is long past: though the old man remembers the long-ago times when he "could tell / A whispering tale in a fair lady's ear," now, alas, his "dancing days" are over (1.5.22–23, 32). But there is also a special subcode that governs the talk and behavior of the young and the powerless; and this juvenile code demands that Romeo and Juliet hear about little else except sex. The lower code is every bit as demanding as the upper code: for instance, the lower code insists that, when a servant encounters a member of a rival family, he has to make childish offensive gestures at him in order to prove the superiority of his own family ("I do bite my thumb, sir"—1.1.45). But chiefly the lower social code requires that every conceivable sentence be reinterpreted as a dirty joke, as if human discourse consisted of nothing except obscene puns. Here, for example, is the joke made by the Nurse (who's in the upper stratum of the lower classes) when she hears Lady Capulet's effusions on the booklikeness of Paris:

> *Lady Cap.* So shall you share all that he doth possess,
> By having him making yourself no less.
> *Nurse.* No less? Nay, bigger! Women grow by men. (1.3.93–95)

Samuel Johnson thought that a central defect of Shakespeare's art was his fondness for puns: "A quibble is to Shakespeare, what luminous vapours are to the traveller; he follows it at all adventures, it is sure to lead him out of his way, and sure to engulf him in the mire. It has some malignant power over his mind."[6] This is going far; but it's true that *Romeo and Juliet* is a play without single entendres.

The code of the young, like the code of the lower classes, entails compulsory punning: erotic haloes backlight the whole text, especially when Mercutio speaks. (Mercutio, of course, does not belong to the lower classes.) Just as the Nurse cannot think of a bump on a child's forehead without thinking of a rooster's testicle (1.3.52), so Mercutio lives in a Beavis and Butthead world where every banana is a penis, every fig a vagina (actually pears and medlars: "O that she were / An open-arse [a soft fruit eaten only at the point of rot], thou a pop'rin pear!"; 2.1.37–38). According to this adolescent code, boys and girls, since they are forcibly restrained from sexual activity—Romeo is, like Juliet, a virgin (3.2.13)—must find a diffuse electric sexuality playing over the whole universe. Mouths that cannot kiss speak words that are simply deflections of kissing.

But the adolescent code and the lower-class code and the upper-class codes all agree, in important ways. To think that a young man is a good potential marriage partner because he will provide substantial sexual pleasure is a love-calculation not much different from such considerations as wealth and social position. It is all part of a utilitarian love code, which measures a suitor according to his usefulness—even his presumed sexual adequacy. It is perhaps strange to think of the gleeful, volatile, boastful, foul-mouthed, rhetorically gifted, mercurial Mercutio as a philistine, but Shakespeare had a reason for making him kin of the Prince. Mercutio is pre-eminently pragmatic, anti-metaphysical, even anti-poetical.

Mercutio's speech about Queen Mab is one of the high points of Shakespeare's art, and yet it is a deconstruction of dreams into emptinesses. It is, by design, a synthesis of nothings, in order to prove the sheer vacuum that lies at the center of Romeo's conception of love:

O then I see Queen Mab hath been with you.
She is the fairies' midwife, and she comes
In shape no bigger than an agot-stone
On the forefinger of an alderman,
Drawn with a team of little atomi
Over men's noses as they lie asleep.
Her chariot is an empty hazelnut,
Made by the joiner squirrel or old grub,
Time out a' mind the fairies' coachmakers.
Her waggon-spokes made of long spinners' legs,
The cover of the wings of grasshoppers;
Her traces of the smallest spider web,
Her collars of the moonshine's wat'ry beams,
Her whip of cricket's bone, the lash of film,
Her waggoner a small grey-coated gnat,
Not half so big as a round little worm
Prick'd from the lazy finger of a maid.
And in this state she gallops night by night
Through lovers' brains, and then they dream of love. (1.4.53–71)

This is an ingenious fantasy designed to dispel fantasy, to mock Romeo with obvious blatant unrealities. Coleridge, in the thirteenth chapter of *Biographia Literaria* (1817), distinguished two image-making faculties in the human mind, which he called Imagination and Fancy:

The primary IMAGINATION I hold to be the living power and prime Agent of all human Perception, and as a repetition in the finite mind of the eternal act of creation in the infinite I AM. The secondary I consider as an echo of the former co-existing with the conscious will . . . It dissolves, diffuses, dissipates, in order to re-create . . . it struggles to idealize and to unify. It is essentially *vital,* even as all objects (*as* objects) are essentially fixed and dead.

FANCY, on the contrary, has no other counters to play with, but fixities and definites. The Fancy is indeed no other than a mode of Memory emancipated from the order of time and space; and blended with, and modified by that empirical phenomenon of the will, which we express by the word CHOICE. But equally with the ordinary memory it must receive all its materials ready made from the law of association.[7]

The Queen Mab speech is one of the most brilliant acts of Fancy in the English language: for it is a deliberate blasphemy against Imagination, a demonstration that highfalutin rhetoric is only a mechanical recombination of existing elements—cheeseparings, lint, discarded nutshells, and other bits of trash. Mercutio appears to be Romeo's friend, but is actually his subtlest enemy: for to attend to Mercutio is to become self-conscious about the artificiality and brittleness of the rhetoric of love—and Romeo needs, above all, to be able to credit the authenticity of what he says to Juliet. Romeo must vehemently assert his sincerity against Mercutio's scoffing precisely because Romeo's own inner Mercutio privately assents to the notion that girls are the interchangeable objects of high rhetoric—in a sense Mercutio *is* Romeo, as Romeo would be if he didn't happen to be in love. Mercutio and Romeo are intimate antagonists, of the sort that Girard relishes in *A Theater of Envy,* so similar to one another that they prove threatening. Romeo can't proceed far with Juliet as long as Mercutio is leering in the background: the two lovers do not consummate their love until after the death of Mercutio. Mercutio's derision is a greater obstacle to love than the wrath of the Capulets.

Mab's speech dismisses itself, and Mercutio, in a later scene, will also dismiss himself: he throws away his life for the sake of an empty game, his swordfight with Tybalt, which is all hip Italian fencing talk and fancy metaphors, as if duelling were a kind of ballet:

> *Tyb.* Mercutio, thou consortest with Romeo—
> *Mer.* Consort! what, dost thou make us minstrels? And thou make minstrels of us, look to hear nothing but discords. Here's my fiddlestick; here's that shall make you dance . . . *Alla stoccato* [at the thrust] carries it away. (3.1.45–49, 74)

Earlier Mercutio remarked that Tybalt "fights as you sing prick-song [printed music], keeps time, distance and proportion; he rests his minim rests, one, two, and the third in your bosom" (2.4.20–23). In a sense Mercutio is a perfect formalist of human life, for whom all is sport, artifice, masque, wit-contest or body-contest. The duel is simply music carried out by other means. Long before Prokofiev's *Romeo and Juliet* ballet, Mercutio understands fencing as a sort of choreography—almost in the manner of a Punch and Judy show, since Mercutio's sword (he claims) enforces specific gestures in Tybalt, makes him dance like a puppet. Like any good Renaissance man, Mercutio has the graces of both warrior and musician. Baldesar Castiglione, whose *Book of the Courtier* (1528; translated into English 1561) was the chief Renaissance handbook of ideal conduct—the most refined statement of the code—thought that a nobleman's stance towards the world should be *sprezzatura,* elegant scorn, nonchalance, an effortless mastery of all arts that shrugs off its own accomplishment; for Castiglione, the height of grace is self-dismissal.[8] Mercutio is, in a somewhat debased form (since he's a compulsive show-off), just such an apprentice scorner. Content means little to him, until he realizes that he's mortally wounded, and cries out in pain ("A plague a' both houses!"—3.1.91, 99–100, 106)—except for that expostulation, Mercutio, like Mab, is all a beautiful, vacant inflection of surface. It is right that he should go joking to his grave ("Ask for me to-morrow, and you shall find me a grave man"—3.1.97–98), for Mercutio is a human jokebook, a thesaurus of puns, a textualized and paginated thing. In the second book of *The Book of the Courtier,* Castiglione provides a taxonomy of puns and quips, ranging from the laboured to the wounding to the elegant, complete with warnings about those inadmissible for court-iers; but Mercutio ranges over the whole span, so nonchalant that good taste itself means nothing to him.

We must consider two more variants of the social code, before we look at Romeo and Juliet themselves: first, the religious code of Friar Lawrence, and second, the law code of the Prince. Both these codes offer certain miti-gations or reliefs from the harshness of the code of the Capulets and the Montagues, the code of endless vendetta. The religious code is embodied by the tolerant, practical, accommodating Lawrence, and is expressed in fairly secular terms, such as *Moderation in all things:* "Love moderately: long love doth so; / Too swift arrives as tardy as too slow" (2.6.14–15). It is likely that Shakespeare did not want the Christian religion to appear in this play in any sort of harsh or austere form, since, by strict Christian accounts, Romeo and Juliet are guilty of grave sins, from breaking the commandment against honoring one's parents, to the mortal sin of suicide: if Shakespeare wished to retain the audience's sympathy, he had to trans-pose the lover's crimes to the classical and pagan sin of immoderate behav-ior. In a play about "star-cross'd lovers" (Prologue 6), lovers who are "fortune's fool[s]" (3.1.136), lovers who consider themselves brought to an unhappy end by blind luck, lovers whose most memorable prayer is "Be fickle, Fortune" (3.5.62), a Christian God has little role to play: the mar-riage ceremony, the play's most Christian moment, seems a frail bulwark against the general willfulness and obstinacy of Fate. Lawrence is a Catho-lic friar, but he manifests some of the Protestant virtues, by siding with the lovers' private and immediate theology, not with the social hierarchy; though Lawrence, like everyone else, is finally unable to provide meaningful assis-tance to them. When he tells Juliet, looking on Romeo's dead body, that "I'll dispose of thee / Among a sisterhood of holy nuns" (5.3.156–57), we see how obtuse Lawrence can be, how far removed from the real, interior drama, despite his desire to be helpful. He relies on prayers and drugs and histrionic tricks, but is equally ineffectual as physician to the soul, physi-cian to the body, and stage manager of a daring flight from parental con-trol. Still, Lawrence's code completely lacks familial partisanship, and thus has offered a partial escape from the code of vendetta.

Another escape from vendetta is found in Prince Escalus's law code. One of the greatest of all dramas, the *Oresteia* of Aeschylus (possibly the Prince's name dimly alludes to this), offers a mythic paradigm for the su-perseding of a barbarous code of vendetta by a true legal system, in which crime is punished by dispassionate authority, not by vengeful kinsman—

the Furies turn Eumenides. But *Romeo and Juliet* does not present the legal system in anywhere so positive a light. Escalus seems an enlightened, prudent, pragmatic ruler, inclined to mercy; Friar Lawrence is impressed by his forbearance in exiling Romeo, instead of killing him:

> Thy fault our law calls death, but the kind Prince,
> Taking thy part, hath rush'd aside the law,
> And turn'd that black word "death" to "banishment."
> This is dear mercy, and thou seest it not. (3.3.25–28)

The Prince, like the Friar, is inclined to mercy, instead of the asperities of strict justice; but he's aware that mercy is by itself inadequate for dealing with human life: "Mercy but murders, pardoning those that kill" (3.1.197). By the end, the futility of both justice and mercy seems clear—the law code was unable to cope with the challenge presented by the love of Romeo and Juliet. Escalus's kinsman Paris, legalistic to a fault, tries to perform a citizen's arrest on the desperate Romeo ("Condemned villain, I do apprehend thee. / Obey and go with me, for thou must die"—5.3.56–57)—and for his trouble Paris gets instantly killed. And Escalus himself is at last helpless, able only to vituperate the Capulets and Montagues and to whip himself for not being a sterner judge: "I for winking at your discords too / Have lost a brace of kinsmen. All are punished" (5.3.294–95). But it's hard to see that less mercy would have helped much. The law code and the vendetta code have both proved useless; Romeo and Juliet managed to pass beyond the proper scope of either.

The Veronese social code, finally, is strong and tenacious but strangely incoherent: its component subcodes can't align themselves into a consistent set of rules for a stable society. Romeo and Juliet provide a comprehensive examination of the code, a test that the code fails to pass. It remains to be seen whether love can construct a viable alternative to govern human conduct.

3. The Code of Love

When we turn to the lovers themselves, we enter a different universe. Self-conscious civilizedness, nippy verbal precisions, continual deference or self-assertion based on hierarchies of control—the whole Veronese social code—must yield to the love code, according to which society exists only as a form of spatial extension into which the beloved can be removed, lost. The first account we have of the new rules by which lovers live can be found in Benvolio's account of how Romeo has shunned all his friends in favor of solitary walks before dawn among the sycamores, and in Montague's response:

Many a morning hath he there been seen,
With tears augmenting the fresh morning's dew,
Adding to clouds more clouds with his deep sighs,
But all so soon as the all-cheering sun
Should in the farthest East begin to draw
The shady curtains from Aurora's bed,
Away from light steals home my heavy son,
And private in his chamber pens himself,
Shuts up his windows, locks fair daylight out,
And makes himself an artificial night. (1.1.131–40)

The lover locks himself inside himself, constitutes his private world, completely exclusive of nature and society alike: he even generates his own private weather, by exhaling clouds of sighs and weeping rivers of tears. Self-involved and melancholy, the lover is a pitiable thing indeed. This is the first tenet of the love code: that the lover dwells on his own planet, a state of emotional self-preoccupation remote from most of human life. Desire, always increasing since its outlets are blocked, carves out and occupies an enormous space inside the desirer, a whole cosmos of insufficiency, absence.

A second tenet becomes clear soon afterward, as Romeo confesses that his beloved ignores him:

                   She'll not be hit
With Cupid's arrow. She hath Dian's wit;
And in strong proof of chastity well arm'd,
From Love's weak childish bow she lives uncharm'd. (1.1.208–11)

Such references to Roman mythology are common in the play, for the planet of love is ruled by pagan deities, not by Christian; the code of love was inscribed not on Moses' tablets or in the gospels but in Ovid's *Amores* and other classical texts—its major commandment is not *Love thy neighbor as thyself* or *Honor the sabbath day to keep it holy* but *Amor vincit omnia.* We soon hear more of Cupid, when Mercutio urges Romeo to dance at the Capulets' ball:

Mer. You are a lover, borrow Cupid's wings
And soar with them above a common bound.
Rom. I am too sore enpierced with his shaft
To soar with his light feathers, and so bound
I cannot bound a pitch above dull woe;
Under love's heavy burthen do I sink. (1.4.17–22)

Mercutio immediately makes a coarse pun, but Romeo refuses to smile: the lover's universe of discourse is heavily sexualized but never obscene—it is a world of tropes that can't easily be dismantled, reduced to some bit of

gynecology. Such figures of speech as Cupid remain about half-way between the Eros of the ancients (so mighty that his arrows could compel
even Apollo to do his will), and our modern sentimentalized Valentine's
day drawing of a cartoon cherub: for Mercutio, Cupid is only concupiscence,
a slightly veiled way of talking about coitus, but for Romeo, Cupid is a
semi-credible god, a name for something intensely significant, for urges
that seem to have some dark referent beyond mere reproductive physiology. Mercutio makes up metaphors and fantasies only to tear them apart,
as with Queen Mab; but Romeo is comfortable living in a domain of detached and stable metaphors, a tropo-sphere.

But classical mythology is not the chief source for the love code of Romeo
and Juliet: the chief source is named explicitly, by Mercutio:

> *Ben.* Here comes Romeo, here comes Romeo.
> *Mer.* Without his roe, like a dried herring: O flesh, flesh, how art thou
> fishified! Now is he for the numbers that Petrarch flow'd in. Laura to
> his lady was a kitchen wench (marry, she had a better love to berhyme
> her), Dido a dowdy, Cleopatra a gipsy. . . . (2.4.36–41)

Petrarch's sonnets to Laura were, in Shakespeare's age, the great verbal
monument to love: they taught many generations of poets the basic conventions of writing love poetry. In a sense, by falling in love Romeo has
abandoned the decorous world ruled by his father and Prince Escalus, in
favor of a spasmodic, lethal world ruled by Francesco Petrarca, where lovers' glances shoot blinding rays, where presence is paradise and absence is
hell, where all that is not fire is ice. In this frantic domain of excluded
middles, Romeo is so comfortably at home that he finds himself compul-
sively speaking sonnets: after Benvolio tells him that, at the Capulets' ball,
Romeo will see such beautiful women that they will make his swan seem a
crow, Romeo fiercely avows his unshakable affection:

> When the devout religion of mine eye
> Maintains such falsehood, then turn tears to fires;
> And these, who, often drown'd, could never die,
> Transparent heretics, be burnt for liars!
> One fairer than my love! The all-seeing sun
> Ne'er saw her match since first the world begun. (1.2.88–93)

This impressive oath, rhymed *ababcc*, forms the sestet of Shakespearean
sonnet. Indeed Romeo, throughout the opening scenes, seems to live inside
the collection of Shakespeare's sonnets (not published until 1609, but often
thought to have been written earlier). This is true of Romeo's themes as
well as his rhyme-patterns: for example, he complains that his cruel fair
deprives not only himself, but the whole of mankind, by remaining chaste:

O, she is rich in beauty, only poor
That, when she dies, with beauty dies her store.
Ben. Then she hath sworn that she will still live chaste?
Rom. She hath, and in that sparing makes huge waste;
For beauty, starv'd with her severity,
Cuts beauty off from all posterity. (1.1.215–20)

A number of Shakespeare's sonnets urge their handsome object to get married and have children, for exactly this reason.

But, of course, both these last quotations concern not Juliet, but Rosaline, Romeo's first inamorata; and therefore they tend to call into question the sincerity of Petrarchan rhetoric, since it is just as usefully applicable to one girl as to another. Romeo's eyes *are* "transparent heretics," since he immediately decides that swan Rosaline is in fact a crow, as soon as he sees Juliet. Romeo must on some level know Mercutio was right about Rosaline, and therefore Romeo's lovely speeches to Juliet are in a sense pre-desecrated, since they (or their like) have already been spoken to Rosaline. The deconstructionist Mercutio continually urges Romeo to understand Petrarchan conceits as a conventional, stylized, boring way of thinking and speaking: here is the disobliging formula by which Mercutio tries to conjure up the absent Romeo:

Romeo! humors! madman! passion! lover!
Appear thou in the likeness of a sigh!
Speak but one rhyme, and I am satisfied;
Cry but "Ay me!", pronounce but "love" and "dove." (2.1.7–10)

For Mercutio, love sonnets are merely clichés. And yet, Romeo, now trying to speak to Juliet, does not repudiate Petrarchan conceits; instead he moves ever deeper into the world of Petrarch and the sonnet:

Rom. If I profane with my unworthiest hand
This holy shrine, the gentle sin is this:
My lips, two blushing pilgrims, ready stand
To smooth that rough touch with a tender kiss.
Jul. Good pilgrim, you do wrong your hand too much,
Which mannerly devotion shows in this:
For saints have hands that pilgrims' hands do touch,
And palm to palm is holy palmers' [pilgrims'] kiss.
Rom. Have not saints lips, and holy palmers too?
Jul. Ay, pilgrim, lips that they must use in pray'r.
Rom. O then, dear saint, let lips do what hands do,
They pray—grant thou, lest faith turn to despair.
Jul. Saints do not move, though grant for prayers' sake.

Rom. Then move not while my prayer's effect I take. . . . [*Kissing her*]
(1.5.93–107)

The first words that Romeo and Juliet exchange in the play constitute a complete Shakespearean sonnet, artfully interwoven by two voices, as if the lovers improvised a complicated stanza form to bind themselves together in poetic form, long before their binding-together in the form of a marriage ceremony. They even play a delicate literary game with the sonnet form: the usual Shakespearean sonnet is rhymed *ababcdcd efefgg*, but they collaborate on a slightly more intricate form (*ababcbcb dedeff*), in which the *b*-sequence is oddly transformed by no-rhymes (*kiss* rhymes with *kiss*; *this* rhymes with *this*)—as if Juliet wishes simply to echo Romeo, to swallow his words, to keep the concentration on the idea of *kiss* as fixed as possible, without slurring it into a related syllable. It is a *pas d'action,* an action sonnet, in that the bending-together of words is fulfilled by a bending-together of lips.

The whole play began with a sonnet, spoken by the Prologue to set the scene of star-crossed love; and in a sense *Romeo and Juliet,* like *Love's Labours Lost,* is a gigantic expansion of sonnet, a sonnet that billows out and slowly deflates, unsonnets itself, returns to the blank verse and prose of common life. In this sense, Shakespeare's play is itself a kind of transgression against itself, in that it aspires to disable itself as a drama, to reconstitute itself as a sort of staged lyric. As far as the lovers are concerned, the dramatic aspects of the play—the feud between Montagues and Capulets, the intrigue to get Juliet married to Paris—are pointless inconveniences; they seek to wrap themselves in the paper of a book of lyric poems. *Romeo and Juliet* could be called an opera without music, in that the drama is continually revised, intensified, betrayed, by the gorgeousness of lyrical metaphors.

At the end of the dialogue-sonnet, Juliet tells Romeo, "You kiss by the book" (1.5.110), a resonant line: she means that he kisses methodically, but she also means that he kisses according to literary conventions. For the rest of the play, the lovers will try to live inside a sonnet, kissing, making love, isolating themselves from other systems of command, according to the well-known recipe of Italian love tropes. In the fifth canto of Dante's *Inferno,* the tourist Dante meets Paolo and Francesca, adulterers who fell into one another's arms because they were spending an idle moment reading aloud stories about Sir Lancelot:

> No greater sadness is
> Than to remember our times of joy
> during our misery . . .
> As we read how he longed for her smile, how delighted
> she felt to be kissed by such lover as he,

this man Paolo, from whom I never shall be divided,
reached out and kissed my mouth all tremblingly.
A Galahaut was the book, and he who wrote it. (5.121–23, 133–37)[9]

Similarly a book—Petrarch's book of sonnets—is a kind of go-between for Romeo and Juliet, giving them access to a totally amorized universe, enabling them to play upon each other's fantasies. They can fall in love instanteously, can conspire to talk sonnets with one another, because they've been reading the same book. The bookishness of this drama can't be exaggerated: if Juliet instantly notices that Romeo kisses by the book, Mercutio will soon note that Tybalt fights by the book (3.1.102; 2.4.21), since Tybalt is au courant with the best recent theories of fencing—*Romeo and Juliet* is a play about reading, and about trying to adapt the practice of life to literary conventions. To some extent, Shakespeare's own book of sonnets acts as a surrogate for Petrarch's, since the lovers continually seem to make allusions to Shakespeare's (still unpublished) sequence of love poems: for example, Romeo, shortly before the catastrophe, remembers a happy dream, in which his own corpse revives from death by means of Juliet's kiss: "Ah me, how sweet is love itself possess'd, / When but love's shadows are so rich in joy!" (5.1.10–11)—lines which seem to point to the haunting couplet from Sonnet 98: "Yet seem'd it winter still, and, you away, / As with your shadow I with these did play." It is as if Shakespeare turned the world of his sonnets inside out, exteriorized it into a drama.

Most Elizabethan sonnet sequences—Spenser's *Amoretti,* Sidney's *Astrophil and Stella,* Daniel's *Delia*—form a kind of lyrico-psychiatric history of the spasms of unrequited (or frustratingly semi-requited) love for a woman. This sort of sonnet sequence has this odd property, that the rhetoric of seduction and sweet complaint, intended to bring the beloved into the lover's arms, ultimately becomes a kind of wall separating the lover from the beloved: one sonnet is an invitation, but a hundred sonnets suggest that the sonneteer has become so engrossed in literature that the beloved is half-forgotten, no matter how loudly he cries out for her. He is addressing himself to his previous poems, not to a woman. But insofar as *Romeo and Juliet* is an everted sonnet sequence, a sonnet sequence with its insides pulled out and put on public display, the co-presence on stage of the two lovers becomes a sort of guarantee that there will be no immuring, no estrangement. Her voice is as intimate, as edgy, as compelling as his. In a sonnet sequence, the beloved is always outside the text—indeed her outsideness is the chief premise of the text; but in *Romeo and Juliet* the lover and the beloved are both figments of words, on the same plane of discourse, in a state of continuous phantasmagorical improvisation based on pre-existent texts; the two lovers, naked textualities, take shelter together within the language, become exposed and vulnerable to one another's speech. Of course Shakespeare's sonnet sequence differs from Spenser's and

Sidney's in that most of the poems apostrophize not a woman but a boy—
an object therefore still further outside any possibility of socially approved
sexual engagement with the male author; but even that aspect is peculiarly
apt to the stage conditions of *Romeo and Juliet,* where Juliet is unmistak-
ably a boy playing the part of a barely adolescent girl.

The love code, as Romeo and Juliet discover, conflicts so grossly with
the social code that it requires a massive adjustment of being. Both lovers
adapt to the new conventions fairly quickly, but with some difficulty.
Rosaline, of course, has given Romeo a head start into the Petrarchan wal-
low, but even he has trouble in figuring out how to behave when the social
code and the love code clash. For example, when Tybalt challenges him,
Romeo exasperates and puzzles the irritable fellow by his bizarre meekness:

> *Tyb.*   . . . thou art a villain.
> *Rom.* Tybalt, the reason that I have to love thee
> Doth much excuse the appertaining rage
> To such a greeting. Villain am I none. (3.1.61–64)

However, since his refusal to fight leads immediately to Mercutio's death,
Romeo rethinks his position, qua lover, on dueling a prospective cousin-
by-marriage, and kills Tybalt. It seems that Romeo's wavering between the
love code and the code of honor leads to the worst possible result.

Juliet, though she can, at the instant of meeting, follow and sing along
with Romeo's sonnet-music, has more difficulty in adapting to the exigencies of the love code. When we first see her, she is playing a role far different from Romeo's: whereas Romeo is mooning over an unrequiting lover,
Juliet is acting as an ideally submissive daughter: after Lady Capulet broaches
the possibility of her marrying Paris, Juliet replies, "But no more deep will
I endart mine eye / Than your consent gives strength to make it fly" (1.3.98–
99). Here there is no hint of dissent from the social code. Even after Juliet
has confessed her all-consuming love for Romeo, during the balcony scene,
Juliet grows abashed as she remembers how far she's deviating from the
prescriptions of the social code that govern the behavior of girls toward
agreeable suitors:

> Fain would I dwell on form, fain, fain, deny
> What I have spoke, but farewell compliment! . . .
>   O gentle Romeo,
> If thou dost love, pronounce it faithfully;
> Or if thou thinkest I am too quickly won,
> I'll frown and be perverse, and say thee nay,
> So thou wilt woo, but else not for the world.
> In truth, fair Montague, I am too fond,
> And therefore thou mayest think my behavior light,

But trust me, gentleman, I'll prove more true
Than those that have more coying to be strange. (2.2.88–89, 93–101)

This is one of the oddest moments of the play: Juliet offers to behave in a manner that caricatures the etiquette book—to frown and play hard to get—if Romeo will agree in advance that it's all an empty ploy to stimulate his desire for her. At this moment the love code starts to usurp the social code, to tear up its conventions and rebuild them according to its greater urgencies.

Juliet's great crisis in the cross-relation of the love code and the social code occurs when the Nurse tells her that Romeo has killed her cousin Tybalt: her first instinct is social and familial, and she curses Romeo:

O nature, what hadst thou to do in hell
When thou didst bower the spirit of a fiend
In mortal paradise of such sweet flesh? (3.2.80–82)

But soon she starts to interrogate her own emotional responses to the Nurse's declaration, "Tybalt is gone, and Romeo banished" (3.2.69), and discovers a surprising truth:

Some word there was, worser than Tybalt's death,
That murd'red me; I would forget it fain,
But O, it presses to my memory
Like damned guilty deeds to sinners' minds:
"Tybalt is dead, and Romeo banished."
That "banished," that one word "banished,"
Hath slain ten thousand Tybalts. (3.2.108–24)

Romeo and Juliet are both poets, in the Petrarchan/Shakespearean school; but here Juliet is also a literary critic of sorts, carefully re-construing the Nurse's sentence in order to interpret it according to the love code, instead of the social code. Soon she becomes adept at an equivocal discourse, which Lady Capulet interprets one way, according to the social code, and Juliet herself interprets in exactly the reverse fashion, according to the love code:

Indeed I never shall be satisfied
With Romeo, till I behold him—dead—
Is my poor heart, so for a kinsman vex'd. (3.5.93–95)

Here is language that punctuates itself in two mutually exclusive ways, according to two mutually exclusive codes: according to the grammar of the social code, the adjective *dead* modifies *Romeo*; according to the grammar of the love code, it modifies *heart*. But, of course, the love code provides a more convincing syntax for the sentence as a whole, and for Juliet's entire emotional life.

Lady Capulet is completely fooled; but other characters catch a glimpse of the weird abstractness of love, its orthogonality from the plane of common life. Romeo, as we have seen, has become his own planet: gravity is not a constant but a variable, changing according to the lover's mood, imparting to Romeo before the Capulets' ball "a soul of lead" (1.4.15), weighing him down as if he were on the planet Jupiter; but, later, gravity can vanish almost completely, as when Friar Lawrence notes that Juliet, about to be married, seems to float in air:

> Here comes the lady. O, so light a foot
> Will ne'er wear out the everlasting flint;
> A lover may bestride the gossamers
> That idles in the wanton summer air,
> And yet not fall; so light is vanity. (2.5.16–20)

Just as the lover generates his own humidity, he generates a whole private biophysics.

When Romeo and Juliet are alone, and can talk to each other without social disguise, completely according to the code of love, we see just how alien love's universe is to more sociable constructions of reality. Even as early as the balcony scene, Romeo tears up the chart of the sky and remaps it utterly:

> But soft, what light through yonder window breaks?
> It is the east, and Juliet is the sun.
> Arise, fair sun, and kill the envious moon . . .
> Two of the fairest stars in all the heaven,
> Having some business, do entreat her eyes
> To twinkle in their spheres till they return.
> What if her eyes were there, they in her head?
> The brightness of her cheek would shame those stars,
> As daylight doth a lamp; her eyes in heaven
> Would through the airy region stream so bright
> That birds would sing and think it were not night. (2.2.2–4, 15–22)

Juliet is first the sun, then two more stars: the lovers constitute their own astronomy, utterly outshining the normal galaxy. Romeo's rhetoric, with its complex interchanging of eyes and stars, works toward a maximum derangement of common notions of mankind's place in the scheme of things: it is as if the universe were turned inside out, shoving the crystalline purity and radiance of the outermost sphere inward to the center, congealed in

Juliet's eyes, while the deadness and inertia of earth (the center, according to Ptolemy) have now become diffused outward, made the property of the heavens. Furthermore, the center and the circumference are now fluent and exchangeable, reversing places by whim. Again and again in this play, the lovers speak of themselves as if they were made of light: Juliet, delirious with sexual anticipation, declares that "Lovers can see to do their amorous rites / By their own beauties" (3.2.8–9); and at the end, in the tomb, Juliet shines like a lantern in the darkness: "here lies Juliet, and her beauty makes / This vault a feasting presence full of light" (5.3.85–86). The lovers' bodies are a kind of phosphorus or radium, glowing eerily with erotic charge.

This swaddling-up of the lovers in their own luminosity, this wrapping of the lovers in their private sky, reaches its climax when the exultant Juliet cries out for night:

> come, loving, black-brow'd night,
> Give me my Romeo, and, when I shall die,
> Take him and cut him out in little stars,
> And he will make the face of heaven so fine
> That all the world will be in love with night,
> And pay no worship to the garish sun. (3.2.20–25)

Romeo will become not just a star but a whole constellation, so brilliant that night and day will be reversed: the daytime code where women are coy and men valiant will be replaced by the nighttime code of love, as Cupid triumphs once and for all over Diana and Mars, the patrons of the social code. It is little wonder that Romeo and Juliet, not quite exhausted even after a night of sexual frenzy, cannot tell whether it is the lark of daylight singing, or the nightingale (3.5.2, 6): love has so confused time and space that the lovers seem to recline in their own interior continuum. Novalis's hymns to night, the second act of *Tristan und Isolde,* the dismemberment of rational time and space achieved by Nietzsche's Dionysus, all seem to lie on the distant horizons of these speeches.

4. Love against Language

To leave the conventions of Verona and enter the conventions of love entails many sorts of confusions, reversals, and definitions. Language itself must be reinvented: instead of a language suitable for condemning or challenging, the lovers need a language suitable for kissing. Arthur Brooke made this clear in a charming couplet—perhaps the only charming couplet—in *Romeus and Juliet*: "A thousand times she kissed, and him unkissed again, / Ne could she speak a word to him, though would she ne'er so fain" (ll.

843–44). But Shakespeare couldn't think of presenting on stage a wedding night that consisted of a mute pantomime of two boys kissing; instead, he had to find a manner of speech that was the verbal equivalent of a pantomime of kissing—a protracted instantaneity of passion. (This deflection of a physical act into words is the same sort of problem that opera composers were later to face: the deflection of a physical act into music.) Normal language pertains to the world of clock time and yardstick space, but the love code enforces unmeasurabilities and immoderations. Love "is too like the lightning" (2.2.118), as Juliet puts it, to be comfortable in the world of normal speech—it is momentaneous, undiscursive, irrational. Of course Romeo and Juliet must die: they could not sustain such a vertigo of passion, such world-undoing spasms of metaphor, over the course of a month, let alone a lifetime: as Friar Lawrence notes,

> These violent delights have violent ends,
> And in their triumph die, like fire and powder,
> Which as they kiss consume. (2.6.9–11)

Love that proclaims itself "infinite as the sea" (2.2.135) must be infinitesimal in duration: it is all poetry, having nothing to do with the prose of home-making, taking out the garbage, arguing about the dog that had an accident on the carpet.

A chief manifestation of love's assault on language is the instability of names:

> O Romeo, Romeo, wherefore art thou Romeo? . . .
> What's Montague? It is not hand nor foot,
> Nor arm nor face, nor any other part
> Belonging to a man. O, be some other name!
> What's in a name? That which we call a rose
> By any other word would smell as sweet. (2.2.33, 40–44)

So Juliet laments, not knowing that Romeo hears her; and Romeo is all too willing to rename himself: "Call me but love, and I'll be new baptiz'd; / Henceforth never will I be Romeo" (2.2.50–51). The code of love tends to scramble the dictionary, tends to re-referentialize language by making every precious word an attribute of one thing only, the beloved; in a sense, Love seems to admit the existence of only one name, one word: the word *love*. Romeo's rebaptism as Love, however, is more easily said than done: though in their ecstasy Romeo and Juliet imagine that Romeo's name is but a superfluous and arbitrary label stuck to him, it turns out that the name Romeo is deeply incorporated into Romeo's flesh—as Romeo learns when he tries to commit an onomastectomy, sheer nomicide:

> O, tell me, friar, tell me
> In what vile part of this anatomy
> Doth my name lodge? . . . [*He offers to stab himself*] (3.3.105–7)

Romeo's social identity is bound up with his name; and social identity is inevitable as long as one lives in society. He cannot expunge his name from the Social Register merely by swearing allegiance to another vision of identity. Still, this is Romeo's most violent attack on the code of honor: for honor is reputation, a field of force that plays about one's name, and to try to gouge name out of flesh is to go as far as one can go toward breaking the iron fetter of the social code.

It is interesting that, at this very moment, when the Nurse prevents Romeo from stabbing him in order to root out his name, Friar Lawrence reproaches him with effeminacy:

> Hold thy desperate hand!
> Art thou a man? Thy form cries out thou art;
> Thy tears are womanish, thy wild acts denote
> The unreasonable fury of a beast.
> Unseemly woman in a seeming man,
> And ill-beseeming beast in seeming both,
> Thou hast amazed me! (3.3.108–14)

The code of honor makes the most strenuous discriminations between man and woman; between man and beast. But as Romeo tries to lose his Romeohood, in order to live by the code of love, he becomes an uncategorizable, androgynous being. According to the love-rhetoric, Juliet is Romeo's soul (2.2.164); and so Romeo's soul grows collaborate, womanish. Sometimes Romeo wishes he had his old honorable masculinity back: after Mercutio's death, for example, Romeo regrets that Juliet's "beauty hath made me effeminate" (3.1.114); but for the most part he seems to accept his new ambisexuality. As Romeo becomes a woman, Juliet, of course, becomes a man: Friar Lawrence urges her to put aside "womanish fear" (4.1.119), and she does exactly that. (Here, as in many places, Shakespeare seems to confess the underlying maleness of the actors who play his female roles: the love code is closely related, one might say, to the acting code, in which all identity is flimsy and easily interchanged.) To lose the name of Romeo or Juliet is to lose the sexual identity that the name's termination grammatically implies.

The play continually experiments with small, local dissolutions of the name Romeo, as if Shakespeare kept toying with the question "What's in a name?" Mercutio breaks *Romeo* down to its first syllable: "[Romeo] without his roe" (2.4.37); and the Nurse notes that Romeo and rosemary begin with the same letter, R, "that's the dog's name" (2.4.209). But whether the name Romeo diminishes to a fish's egg, or a mere rrrrruff, it's still hard to lose. It's possible that Juliet also puns on the first letter of her name, since in the Elizabethan alphabet *I* and *J* are the same letter:

> Hath Romeo slain himself? Say thou but ay,
> And that bare vowel *I* shall poison more
> Than the death-darting eye of cockatrice.
> I am not I, if there be such an ay. (3.2.45–48)

Juliet's *I* and Romeo's *are* cling to them; and whenever they temporarily rejoin the orbit of human society, their names start to grow vivid. For example, when Romeo starts to make dirty jokes, bantering in the old accustomed way, Mercutio points out how Romeoid he's acting:

> Why, is not this better now than groaning for love? Now art thou sociable, now art thou Romeo; now art thou what thou art, by art as well as by nature, for this drivelling love is like a great natural [fool] that runs lolling up and down to hide his bable [fool's wand] in a hole. (2.4.88–93)

This is one of the most telling speeches in the play: for, from Mercutio's worldly, ironic perspective, the code of love is simply a form of willed idiocy. The idiot and the lovesick man have this in common: they babble, for they have no articulate, sensible speech; in *A Midsummer Night's Dream,* Theseus, a somewhat Mercutio-like character, indicates some other points of comparison between lunatic and lover.

Love's idiocy, love's defeat of logic and language, can be seen most powerfully on the level of tropes. We've already seen how trope-driven love's discourse is, how credulous of pagan gods, how unwilling to sink to commonplace referents. But there is one special trope characteristic of the love code: the *oxymoron.* Mercutio makes obscene puns; Romeo, by contrast, makes oxymorons, even during his very first speech in the play, when he expostulates over the stupidity of the Montague-Capulet street brawl (we must remember that Rosaline is, like Juliet, a Capulet—Romeo seems attracted to danger):

> Here's much to do with hate, but more with love.
> Why then, O brawling love! O loving hate!
> O any thing, of nothing first create!
> O heavy lightness, serious vanity,
> Misshapen chaos of well-seeming forms,
> Feather of lead, bright smoke, cold fire, sick health. (1.1.175–80)

The social code tends to separate, to make distinctions, to create hierarchies; the love code crushes distinctions into paradox. Love's universe is so eager to effect a convergence of extremes that love and hate themselves become undifferentiated intensities—this is why Juliet, after hearing of Tybalt's death, can correctly call Romeo a "fiend angelical!" (3.2.75). *Romeo and Juliet,* with its flocks of swans and crows (1.2.87; 1.5.48; 3.2.19, 76), with its first glimpse of Juliet as a "rich jewel in an Ethiop's ear" (1.5.46), is a drama of extremely high contrasts in black and white; but all these polarities tend to collapse into a state of tense equivalence. Throughout the play, the characters comment on the uncanny intimacy of hate and love—these antonyms appear often in the closest proximity: "My only love sprung from my only hate!" (Juliet, 1.5.138); "thankful even for hate that is meant love" (Juliet, riddling her parents, 3.5.149—well might Capulet exclaim, "chopp'd logic!"). No wonder that the musicians, puzzling about what sort of music to play for a wedding that has turned into a funeral, can think only of a "merry dump" (4.5.107). Romeo and Juliet seem to exert a field of force that distorts normal modes of thinking and forces all the characters, even the most obtuse, to enter a world of contradiction; they leave knots of paradox in the air around them. Even Friar Lawrence is caught up in the general oxymoronity, as he enters the orbit of the love code: when he gathers herbs, he reflects that every medicine is a poison, and that all virtue and vice are oddly commingled, inextricable: "The earth that's nature's mother is her tomb; / What is her burying grave, that is her womb" (2.3.9–10).

The rhyme of *tomb/womb* is at the center of the love-poetics of the play. As we come closer and closer to the heart of the tragedy, we approach a condition of *Liebestod,* Love-Death, a condition of exchange, even transvestism, between Eros and Thanatos. In one of Aesop's fables, later turned into a splendid masque by Shirley (with operatically full music by Matthew Locke and Christopher Gibbons), Love and Death get their quivers mixed up, and so Love's arrows result in a pile of handsome young corpses, while Death's arrows result in a gang of old geezers running around the fields trying to hug one another. The language derangements of *Romeo and Juliet* also culminate in a systematic confusion of Love and Death: "I'll to my wedding-bed, / And death, not Romeo, take my maidenhead!" (3.2.136–37)—and soon Juliet tries to literalize this metaphor by pleading with Friar Lawrence to "bid me go into a new-made grave, / And hide with a dead man in his shroud" (4.1.84–85). The woman whose greatest joy was hugging Romeo now finds herself begging to hug some anonymous corpse. But this is only the beginning of a continual surrogation of love by death: as she approaches a real tomb she starts to thrill with fear at the thought of going mad, "And in this rage, with some great kinsman's bone, / As with a club, dash out my desp'rate brains" (4.3.53–54)—the final revenge of the social code on the illicit lover. Here we see Juliet understanding that her repertoire of play-identities includes not only intensely erotic roles, but Death itself, and Death's victim. Later, when Juliet seems dead, Capulet is struck with horror at the thought of a daughter "deflowered" by Death, a villain pictured as a kind of serial rapist (4.5.37). Romeo, too, plays with the same skein of entangled death-love, love-death: when he hears of Juliet's (false) death, he immediately seeks poison—"Well, Juliet, I will lie with thee to-night" (5.1.34); as he pries open Juliet's tomb, he calls it "Thou detestable maw, thou womb of death" (5.3.45); in the tomb, Romeo, jealous of Death itself, imagines Juliet as Persephone, a kind of love-slave or concubine in the underworld:

> Shall I believe
> That unsubstantial Death is amorous,
> And that the lean abhorred monster keeps
> Thee in dark to be his paramour? (5.3.102–5)

By dying, Romeo can *become* Death, in a sense; can be Juliet's last, most intently commingling lover. With death, as with love, one can reach the highest imaginable intensity of sensation—and Romeo and Juliet are, in a sense, connoisseurs of extreme feeling-states, craving the least safe kind of sex imaginable. If, in the language of the love code, all words tend to mean love, there is an inevitable slipping of reference, a sort of linguistic entropy, as *love* grows synonymous with *death*.

The name *Liebestod* is associated with high Romantic art, for it is the name that Liszt gave to the final scene in Wagner's opera *Tristan und Isolde* (1865), where Isolde, standing over the corpse of Tristan, liquidates herself in immoderate modulations of love. And as we explore the deeper mysteries of Shakespeare's love-rhetoric we seem to be in the domain of Romanticism. Coleridge delighted in the play's oxymorons, and regarded Romeo's lines about the feather of lead and the bright smoke as an example of the highest powers of literary imagination: in these lines we have

> an effort of the mind, when it would describe what it cannot satisfy itself with the description of, to reconcile opposites and qualify contradiction, leaving a middle state of mind more strictly appropriate to the imagination than any other, when it is, as it were, hovering between images. As soon as it is fixed on one image, it becomes understanding; but while it is unfixed and wavering between them, attaching itself permanently to none, it is imagination. . . . The grandest efforts of poetry are where the imagination is called forth, not to produce a distinct form, but a strong working of the mind, still offering what is repelled, and again creating what is again rejected; the result being what the poet wishes to impress, namely, the substitution of a sublime feeling of the unimaginable for a mere image. (*Lectures upon Shakespeare VII*, 1811–12)[10]

Coleridge, speaking as a great poet of the Romantic movement, was inclined to applaud (at least as long as Christian values remained safe) all dismantling of rational category, all smearing of the ink of old codes: the purity and force of love seemed to undo the whole stale antithesis-driven universe. But was Shakespeare a Romantic? Did Shakespeare in any sense recommend or seek to glorify the actions or the language of Romeo and Juliet? Or did Shakespeare agree with Arthur Brooke, who wrote in the brief preface to *Romeus and Juliet*:

> The glorious triumph of the continent man upon the lusts of wanton flesh, encourageth men to honest restraint of wild affections; the shameful and wretched ends of such as have yielded their liberty to foul desires teach men to withhold themselves from the headlong fall of loose dishonesty. . . . And to this end, good reader, is this tragical matter written, to describe unto thee a couple of unfortunate lovers, thralling themselves to unhonest desire; neglecting the authority and advice of parents and friends; conferring their principal counsels with drunken gossips and superstitious friars . . . attempting all adventures of peril for th' attaining of their wished lust . . . abusing the honorable name of lawful marriage to cloak the shame of stolen contracts; finally by all means of unhonest life hasting to more unhappy death.

For the Romantics, the story of Romeo and Juliet recommends the code of love, full of confusions of fire and ice; but for Brooke, the story recommends a code of conduct that casts a cold eye on love.

Shakespeare certainly put more effort into devising the speeches of Romeo and Juliet than, say, those of Capulet and his wife; but that doesn't mean that he felt that the love code is a plausible way of organizing human relationships. We have seen the inadequacy of the old social code, its crudity, its faulty psychology and incoherent ethics. It is no surprise that Verona has fallen into an interminable state of civil war, governed by such a helpless code. But it's doubtful that Petrarch can supply a reasonable alternative. The universe of Romeo and Juliet is, in its way, as heartless and brutal as that of the social code: it seeks to unrealize, to dismiss, most of human life. Note that when the Nurse decides, after Romeo has killed Tybalt, that the love code has failed to make Juliet happy, the Nurse retreats to the only other code she knows, the social code:

> I think it best you married with the County [Paris].
> O he's a lovely gentleman!
> Romeo's a dishclout to him. (3.5.217–19)

Juliet instantly considers the Nurse a traitor: "Ancient damnation! O most wicked fiend!" (3.5.235). This judgment is far harsher than any of Prince Escalus's: the field on which the rules of Petrarch hold is exclusive, suspicious, small, and always getting smaller, as Romeo and Juliet push away everyone who could conceivably assist them, first the Nurse, then Friar Lawrence (4.3.24—Juliet wonders whether Lawrence has given her a real poison instead of the drug that will produce a simulation of death). It is impossible to imagine that Shakespeare hoped that we would all regulate our lives according to the governance of sonnets: a fully Petrarchized society would be in a state of continual warfare, just like Verona.

And yet, if neither the love code nor the social code can alone suffice, it's possible that the social code could improve itself by trying to understand and to embrace the formalized anarchy of young love; and possible that the love code could improve itself by trying to understand the general inertia, ignorant typology, and punctilious arrogance of the social code. One of the puzzles of *Romeo and Juliet* is, why did Shakespeare continue the last scene so long-windedly after the deaths of the lovers? As Dr. Johnson put it, "Narration in dramatic poetry is naturally tedious, as it is unanimated and inactive. . . . Shakespeare found it an encumbrance, and instead of lightening it by brevity, endeavoured to recommend it by dignity and splendour."[11] Almost every director who emends the play cuts out, or even rewrites, much of the last 150 lines; and yet Shakespeare often has a purpose in his tedium. Why would any spectator want to hear Friar Lawrence speak a long, long, dutiful plot summary of exactly those events that have been excitingly presented on stage? Perhaps the answer is that Shakespeare wanted Romeo and Juliet to move beyond drama into narrative, in order to suggest that their story could be integrated into the other stories that make up our lives; Prince Escalus leaves us with the hope that this extraordinary, irrational love-narrative might pass into an example, and that this example might help to rectify some of the errors of the social code. For most of its duration, *Romeo and Juliet* attempts to transgress itself by wrenching drama into an expansion of a sonnet; but as it concludes, the play attempts to transgress itself by smoothing the drama into the (slightly too mellifluous and pat) narrative cadences of Friar Lawrence's voice. At the very end, we hear that Montague is going to build a "statue in pure gold" (5.3.299) of Capulet's daughter, and that Capulet will do the same for Montague's son. Juliet had hoped that Romeo would survive after death as a heavenly constellation (3.2.22), but instead they both survive only as a story, and as a pair of statues: entities in the world of human society, not in the world of Petrarchan fantasy, reminders of something precious to mankind that resists easily assimilation into books of law and codes of honor.

From Shakespeare to Berlioz

1. The Afterlife of Romeo and Juliet

Shakespeare's theatres all became bare ruined choirs in 1642, when Parliament dissolved them during the English Civil War; and after Oliver Cromwell's Republic ended, and the theatres reopened in 1660, Shakespeare's plays began a long reassimilation into the cultural consciousness of England. Juliet, who died a boy in Shakespeare's day, awoke and found herself transsexualized into a woman—for now actresses were permitted on stage, on a stage itself much changed, for the bare platform of the old theatre had been replaced by a stage with a proscenium arch and elaborate backdrops. And Shakespeare's words also started to mutate in their Restoration afterlife, as they were reconfigured into a locus of multimedia spectacles.

Shakespeare's theatre had been, to a certain degree, an inexpensive popular theatre—the Curtain or the Globe had none of the elaborately painted backdrops, the architectural extravaganzas, of the sort that Inigo Jones designed for the court masques of Ben Jonson. Shakespeare's approach to dramaturgy is often fluid, quasi-improvisatory; his stage is often a melange of sub-stages, in which the bare expanse of flooring can represent, almost at the same time, a battlefield, a court, a forest, a bedchamber:

> Can this cockpit hold
> The vasty fields of France? Or may we cram
> Within this wooden O the very casques
> That did affright the air at Agincourt? (*Henry V*, Prologue 11–14)

Yes, all that, and more, much more. But the Restoration theatre had little interest in the jump-cuts, the startling mutations of place, featured in the Elizabethan theatre; it wanted spectacle, and the slower stage-rhythms that the machinery of spectacle necessarily entail. And it wanted music: not just the solitary lute-player / singer who can be hustled quickly on-and off-stage, but fully worked-out scenes, sometimes with choruses, duets, and a small orchestra. In this manner Shakespeare's text tended to become the recitative connecting one stupendous set-piece to the next. The semi-opera, or the quarter-opera, took shape, partly out of the desire to reproject Shakespeare onto an alien theatrical world.

Shakespeare slowly shifted into a sort of opera librettist, but a librettist who needed help from local experts. John Dryden regarded the 1674 version of *The Tempest* as the first English opera; and Nahum Tate, the very fellow who wrote the libretto for the first English opera (*not* semi-opera) that is still frequently performed—Purcell's *Dido and Aeneas* (written during the 1680s)—also was the man who wrote a new ending for *King Lear,* in which Cordelia revives and marries Edgar, Lear is restored to his throne, and all concludes well—an ending that remained popular for decades to come.

But evidently no one wanted an ending to *Romeo and Juliet* in which Romeo lifts the poison to his lips, then notices Juliet faintly stirring, throws away the vial before drinking it, hugs her madly, and persuades old Capulet that the murderer of Tybalt and Paris would make a sober, reliable husband for his daughter. *King Lear* is a tragedy, whether or not a *deus ex machina* can impose a happy ending; but *Romeo and Juliet* becomes a pointless thing, a romantic comedy crammed with corpses, if the lovers are allowed to unite in the end. So we must posit further rewriting: the text must somehow show that Tybalt and Paris aren't really dead, either, but only badly wounded, capable of seeing the error of their ways and blessing the marriage of Romeo and Juliet—Ah, Romeo, [*coughs*] I see it clear, thou art a better man than I. In fact (as many critics have noticed) the endpoint of the comic metamorphosis of *Romeo and Juliet* is simply the Pyramus and Thisby episode of *A Midsummer Night's Dream,* a farce in which the actors roar gently so as not to make the ladies in the audience a-feared, and the actors whisper aside that no one really gets hurt, even if stage blood is spilled everywhere.

So, if *Romeo and Juliet* was to be mollified by a taste that considered itself more refined, less extravagant and harsh than Shakespeare's, the maceration of the text had to proceed in other areas. It turned out that posterity—first in Thomas Otway's version (1680), then in David Garrick's (1748)—decided that the death scene was the unsatisfactory, too-unhappy part of the play: and it could be softened simply by allowing the two lovers a final goodbye in the course of a spoken duet—a sort of operatization of the text. It seemed that Shakespeare muffed the ending by not seeing the choice dramatic possibilities for dialogue between the dying Romeo and the revived Juliet.

In some ways Shakespeare's handling of the lovers' deaths (5.3.120–70) really is odd, abrupt, almost brusque. The poison (unusually, for stage poisons) works instantly: Romeo drinks it and drops dead beside Juliet; by clockwork precision of contrivance, Romeo's death is the cue for Friar Lawrence's entry and Juliet's rousing. She "dies," then he dies; he dies, then she dies. The avoidance of any dialogue between the lovers in this scene was clearly a conscious choice: for example, in *Othello*—in a scene much derided by Voltaire—Shakespeare allowed Othello to smother Desdemona

(a species of murder that one would expect to be immediately effective, unlike poison), but Desdemona lingers on for a few minutes, to chat with her husband. Why did Shakespeare deny his lovers the leniency of farewell?

Again, it is possible to find an answer in the conventions of love sonnets. We've seen that *Romeo and Juliet* is a drama confected in order to invent an artificial venue in which the sonneteer and his beloved can coinhabit a world—as opposed to the usual conditions of sonnet-life, where the beloved is at a far remove, and usually getting, as the sequence evolves, still farther. But by the end of the play, the normal conditions of love poetry are starting to reassert themselves, in a sinister way. To write a poem to a woman is to objectify her—to substitute for the living woman an artifice made purely of words, like the False Florimell of Spenser's *The Faerie Queene*, a gynoid synthesized out of various remote ingredients by a witch, in order to trick a noble lover:

> The substance, whereof she the bodie made,
>> Was purest snow in massie mould congeald . . .
>> The same she tempred with fine Mercury,
>> And virgin wex, that never yet was seald,
>> And mingled them with perfect vermily,
> That like a lively sanguine it seem'd to the eye.
>
> In stead of eyes two burning lampes she set
>> In silver sockets, shyning like the skyes,
>> And a quicke moving Spirit did arret
>> To stirre and roll them, like a womans eyes;
>> In stead of yellow lockes she did devise,
>> With golden wyre to weave her curled head;
>> Yet golden wyre was not so yellow thrise
>> As *Florimells* fair haire: and in the stead
> Of life, she put a Spright to rule the carkasse dead. (3.8.6–7)

The snow is pure, the mercury is fine, the wax is virgin, and the creature derived from them is a blank, a zero—a nonentity put into a hectic simulation of life by the figures of speech of love poets. Spenser's snow-woman is made by the same recipe as those famous engravings of women drawn as literalizations of amorous similes: for example, the picture (figure 1) in Charles Sorel's *The extravagant shepherd* (1654), which shows a sort of gorgon with round tooth-balls to represent pearls, actual roses growing out of her cheeks, suns streaming darts from her eyesockets, a network of wires as a wig, and the globe's eastern and western hemispheres clapped onto her chest for breasts. Juliet, whose eyes flew into the heavens, while two stars dawdled on each side of her nose, was always in danger of perish-

ing into a grotesque, an unseemly compound of tropes. In this sense, Romeo
himself was the potion that induced her to a mock death: the poetry he
devised had a certain tendency to chill her, to abstract and alienate her, as
the rhetoric of seduction grew self-engrossed. When Romeo and Juliet met,
she seemed able to dwell with him inside a sonnet; by the end, she has come
to obey the rule of distancing that sonnets tend to impose upon their objects. Why was Romeo not allowed to say goodbye to Juliet?—because
insofar as she was the artifact of Romeo's words, he never knew her in the
first place, except as a latently moribund thing, a pseudo-corpse.

But the passage of time made Juliet less interesting as an extrapolation
of the ideal beloved of sonnet-writers, and more interesting as an erotic
object on the stage. Shakespeare's Juliet, derived from the conventions of
the love lyric, is a thing of fire and ice, virginal yet hoarse from venery, a
staged oxymoron; but the seventeenth-and eighteenth-century revisers im-
posed a moral clarity and aesthetic singleness-of-effect on Shakespeare's
paradoxicalities, his odd sort of dramatic aporia. As Norman Rabkin puts
it, "The radical modifications . . . consist not so much of the neoclassic
regularization one might expect as of attempts to focus the problematic
qualities of the tragedies, to tame them and make them vehicles for providing comfort and reassurance and lucid understanding to their audience."[1]
Rabkin goes on to cite Dryden's definition of character: "A character .
. . is a composition of qualities which are not contrary to one another
in the same person"[2]—a definition which might suggest that (for
Shakespeare's regularizers) Shakespeare's plays contained scarcely any
characters, since contradictory traits are a feature of most the *dramatis
personae* we best remember. The masks needed to be ironed into
straighter shapes.

As Juliet simplified into an ingenue, Romeo bulked out, grew reliable
and dutiful. By the middle of the eighteenth century, the celebrated actor
David Garrick—wearing clothes of the sort we see in pictures of George
Washington—played Romeo opposite a Juliet wearing a long flowing dress
with a good deal of *décolletage*. Garrick cut the play in order to heighten
the purity and noble sentiment of the two lovers: for one thing, he elimi-
nated Rosaline, thereby rendering Romeo's love-rhetoric to Juliet unim-
peachably sincere. And he rewrote the death scene to include the warm
sobbing farewell that Shakespeare refused to his lovers—a scene full of
Dramatic Irony because Romeo forgets he's swallowed poison, and Juliet
confuses Romeo with Paris:

Romeo. . . . Soft! soft! She breathes and stirs! [Juliet *wakes.*]

Juliet. Where am I? Defend me, powers!
Romeo. She speaks, she lives! And we shall still be blessed!

My kind propitious stars o'erpay me now
For all my sorrows past. Rise, rise, my Juliet,
And from this cave of death, this house of horror,
Quick let me snatch thee to thy Romeo's arms,
There breathe a vital spirit in thy lips
And call thee back to life and love! [*Takes her hand.*]
Juliet. Bless me! How cold it is! Who's there?
Romeo. Thy husband.
It is thy Romeo, love; raised from despair
To joys unutterable! Quit, quit this place,
And let us fly together. [*Brings her from the tomb.*]
Juliet. Why do you force me so? I'll ne'er consent.
My strength my fail me, but my will's unmoved.
I'll not wed Paris: Romeo is my husband.
Romeo. Her senses are unsettled. Restore 'em, heavn!
Romeo is thy husband; I am that Romeo.
Not all th' opposing powers of earth or man
Can break our bonds or tear thee from my heart.

But soon this happy idyll ends, as the poison makes Romeo's face grow pale, his eyes swim:

Romeo. . . . Fate brought me to this place to take a last,
Last farewell of my love and with thee die.
Juliet. Die! Was the friar false?
Romeo. I know not that.
I thought thee dead. Distracted at the sight,
Fatal speed! drank poison, kissed thy cold lips,
And found with thy arms a precious grave.
But in that moment—O—
Juliet. And did I wake for this?
Romeo. My powers are blasted.
Twixt death and life I'm torn, I am distracted!
But death's strongest—and must I leave thee Juliet?
O, cruel cursed fate! in sight of heaven—[3]

It is easy to sneer at Garrick's blank verse, with its "Soft! soft!" and "Quit, quit" and "Rise, rise" and "last, last," its drear tombs and joys unutterable—well indeed might Garrick say (in an ugly half-rhyme), "My powers are blasted! . . . I am distracted!" The whole scene could be put in the mouths of Pyramus and Thisby, with little impropriety. But it must be remembered that Garrick's scene was often considered, for more than a century, not only an indispensable part of the play, but one of the highlights.

2. La lance branlée

As Romeo and Juliet developed in time, changing from figments derived from lyric poetry into sentimental adolescents, they also migrated through space, returning to the Romance languages from which they came. Shakespeare had found the characters and plot in a long edifying poem by Arthur Brooke, who in turn had inherited the story from a number of French and Italian sources; but when, in the eighteenth century, Romeo and Juliet returned to their native lands, they came speaking an English accent, at once familiar and strange.

For the most influential Continental critic of the eighteenth century, Voltaire, Shakespeare was the enemy of dramatic art. Voltaire lived for a time in England, and had far more experience with Shakespeare than most of his European contemporaries; and what he found in Shakespeare was simply chaos—a barbarous disregard for the unities of time and place, and a vulgar love for mixing the noble and the ignoble. Voltaire cringed to hear the jokes of Roman cobblers in a scene from *Julius Caesar* where Brutus and Cassius discoursed; and he was sickened by the gravediggers in *Hamlet,* singing ballads as they dug up old skulls. According to Voltaire's *Letters Concerning the English Nation* (1734), Shakespeare was a genius of disgust:

> *Shakespear* boasted a strong, fruitful Genius: He was natural and sublime, but had not so much as a single Spark of good Taste, or knew one Rule of the Drama. . . . the great Merit of this Dramatic Poet has been the Ruin of the English Stage. There are such beautiful, such noble, such dreadful Scenes in this Writer's monstrous Farces, to which the Name of Tragedy is given, that they have always been exhibited with great Success. Time, which only gives Reputation to Writers, at last makes their very Faults venerable. Most of the whimsical, gigantic Images of this Poet, have, thro' Length of Time . . . acquir'd a Right of passing for sublime.[4]

But in a century's time, these censures would start to sound like praise. When the Romantic movement began, Shakespeare's neglect of the classical unities, his taste for the whimsical and monstrous, would seem like a heroic repudiation of stale Art in favor of abundant Nature.

For our purposes, the key year for the French Romantic revaluation of Shakespeare is 1827. In October of that year, Victor Hugo published his play *Cromwell* together with its famous preface: a paean to Shakespeare and a manifesto of Romantic drama. The main thesis of the preface concerned the virtue of the mixed. Hugo recommended a mixture of verse and prose, the tragic and the comic, the sublime and the grotesque—since, according to the Christian religion, man is intrinsically a mixture of pure soul and transitory flesh. This leads Hugo to a ringing defense of the ugly as a necessary aspect of art—a defense that will be taken up again and again through the nineteenth century, by Flaubert, Chekhov, and many others, and will become a prime tenet of Expressionism in the twentieth century. And the locus classicus of the ugly is the canon of Shakespeare:

> . . . as a point of view with respect to the sublime, as a means of contrast, the grotesque is (according to us) the richest source that nature can open to art. Rubens doubtless understood this, when he was pleased to mix with his unfoldings of royal pomp, coronations, splendid ceremonies, some hideous figure of a court dwarf. This sort of universal beauty which antiquity solemnly spread out over everything wasn't without monotony; the same impression, always repeated, can at length be fatiguing. The sublime on top of the sublime produces a poor contrast, and one needs to rest from everything, even from the beautiful. It seems, on the contrary, that the grotesque is a stopping-place, a term of comparison, a point of departure from which one is lifted toward the beautiful with a fresher and more excited perception. The salamander throws the undine into relief; the gnome makes the sylph beautiful. . . .
>
> . . . in [Christian] poetry, while the sublime will represent the soul just as it is, [the grotesque] will play the role of the human beast. The first type, disengaged from every impure bond, will carry with it every charm, every grace, every beauty: it must create Juliet, Desdemona, Ophelia. The second will take every ridiculous thing, every infirmity, every ugliness. To this division of humanity and creation will come passions, vices, crimes; there will be the lecher, the groveler, the glutton, the miser, the traitor, the bungler, the hypocrite; there will be by turns Iago, Tartufe, Basile; Polonius, Harpagon, Bartholo; Falstaff, Scapin, Figaro. There is only one type of the beautiful, but the ugly has a thousand types. The beautiful . . . is merely form considered in its simplest relation, in its most absolute symmetry, in the most intimate harmony. . . . It offers to us a finished ensemble, but circumscribed, as we ourselves are circumscribed. What we call the ugly, on the contrary, is a detail of a great ensemble that escapes our grasp, and which harmonizes itself, not with man, but with creation in its entirety. That is why it presents us ceaselessly with new aspects, but incomplete aspects.[5]

Beauty is narrow, exclusive, thin-lipped, thin-hipped, a little tedious, faintly repellent; ugliness is rich and diversified and evil and generous, life itself. It is little wonder that Hugo would come to write a drama in which the star player would be a hunchbacked jester (Rigoletto, as Verdi renamed him); or to write a novel in which gypsies mutilate children in order to make them more compelling objects of pity when begging for alms: for beauty is locked in itself, while ugliness is connected to the whole of mankind, and the whole of the inanimate universe as well. Through pondering the ugly we know what it feels like to be a misshapen rock, or a sand dune, or a heap of logs, or the solar system. Though Hugo loosely equates the sublime with the beautiful, it is the ugly that is (as Burke or Kant would have understood the term) sublime.

The ramifications of this aesthetic position on *Romeo and Juliet* are clear. The eighteenth century wanted more Juliet, and a more pathetic Juliet; the nineteenth century wanted more Nurse, more Mercutio, more Friar Lawrence, even—more of the gargoyles that channel the dramatic flow around the central intrigue. As an advanced Romantic complained after hearing, in 1831, Bellini's recent opera *I Capuleti e i Montecchi*:

> What a disappointment!!! in the libretto there is no ball at the Capulets', no Mercutio, no chatterbox nurse, no grave, calm hermit, no balcony scene, no sublime monologue for Juliet as she receives the vial from the hermit, no duet in the cell between the exiled Romeo and the desolated hermit; no Shakespeare, nothing; a failed work.[6]

The writer of this passage was Hector Berlioz, who, eight years later, would compose the most searching musical work ever written on the Romeo and Juliet theme.

This leads us to one of my main arguments: the dramatic symphony *Roméo et Juliette* could be considered a revision of Shakespeare through the premises of Victor Hugo. Berlioz's (somewhat unfair) complaints about the monotony of effeminate gorgeous melodies in Bellini's opera recall Hugo on the *ennui* of unrelieved beauty; and Berlioz took care to shape his *Roméo et Juliette* as a dialectic of the beautiful and the grotesque, exactly as Hugo recommended. Berlioz, like Hugo's Shakespeare, had a genius for the mixed mode.

In addition to the preface to *Cromwell*, the year 1827 also saw the visit to Paris of a troupe of British actors, playing Shakespeare, in English. This venture was surprisingly successful; and many of the best minds and subtlest temperaments in France, including Delacroix, Dumas, de Vigny, and Berlioz, were suddenly full of Shakespeare. The impresario did not consider his company especially talented, and tried to enrich it with visits from established actors, such as Edmund Kean and Charles Kemble. Kemble arrived, but was unwilling to play Romeo until a decent Juliet could be found; meanwhile, he agreed to play Hamlet, since he thought Ophelia a trifling role that anyone could handle. In this manner Paris heard the Ophelia of a little-known actress, whose Irish accent had seemed, to British ears, deplorable: Harriet Smithson. But her accent was no impediment in Paris, where many in the audience, including Berlioz, didn't know English in the first place: and her recklessness and mad grace, her beauty and control of gesture, made her a star overnight. As Berlioz wrote:

I come now to the greatest drama of my life. I won't tell all its sad peripeties. I will limit myself to saying this: an English troupe came to Paris to give some performances of the dramas of Shakespeare, then completely unknown to the French public. I attended the first performance of *Hamlet* at the Odéon. I saw in the role of Ophelia Henriette Smithson, who, five years later, became my wife. The effect of her prodigious talent, or rather her dramatic genius, on my imagination and on my heart, is comparable only to the upheaval worked on me by Shakespeare himself—whose worthy interpreter she was. I can say nothing more.

Shakespeare, falling unforeseen, struck me like lightning. His bolt, opening for me the heaven of art with a sublime riot, lit up the most distant depths. . . . at the same time I took the measure of the immense ridiculousness of the ideas concerning Shakespeare that Voltaire had popularized.[7]

Berlioz went on to say that he was prostrate from shock, in a condition of intense *chagrin* combined with a pathological state of nerves. But soon he collected himself, and went to see Harriet Smithson's Juliet—the management now had no qualms about allowing her to play the role:

After the melancholy . . . after the dark clouds, the icy winds of Denmark, to be exposed to the ardent sun, the perfumed nights of Italy, to be present at the spectacle of this love quick as thought, burning as lava, imperious, irresistible, immense, and pure and beautiful as the smile of the angels, at these furious scenes of vengeance, at these distraught embraces, at these desperate struggles of love and death, it was too much. And so, by the third act, breathing with difficulty, and suffering as if an iron hand had squeezed my heart, I said to myself with utter conviction: Ah! I am lost. . . . An English critic said last winter in the *Illustrated London News* that after seeing Juliet played by Miss Smithson I cried out: "I will marry this woman! and out of this drama I will write my largest symphony!" I did these things, but I said nothing like that. . . . what my overwhelmed soul didn't even permit itself to dream, has become a reality.[8]

Berlioz wrote his *Mémoires* many years after the events described, but his prose is remarkably vivid: indeed the act of writing seems almost a sort of auto-hypnosis, in which the acute physiological crisis of his response to Shakespeare, and to Smithson, is re-created.

To fall in love with an actress is to fall in love, not just with one role, but with the whole range of roles that she has played, or might play. It is an unfocusable sort of affection, directed not at a particular set of personality traits, but at a field of possibility. (Oscar Wilde's *The Picture of Dorian*

Gray, a novel in which the chief female character is an actress, is especially good in portraying this histrionic nebulousness of desire.) It is the intimate psychic equivalent of the mixed mode recommended by Hugo: for to love an actress is to love the pure and the grotesque, the ingenue and the mad-woman; to love a teasing and pregnant locus of selves; to love all women instead of any one woman; to love the universe. Off stage, Harriet Smithson turned out to be a fussy, mother-dominated creature, older than Berlioz, saddled with mountains of debt, somewhat lame after breaking her ankle, altogether a disappointing wife; but any contraction to a finite identity would have seemed a betrayal of the omnisentient incarnations of Shakespeare's imagination that Berlioz glimpsed on stage. The Romantic poet Keats (born eight years before Berlioz) applauded Shakespeare for his *negative capability,* his indistinctness and motility of being—for Keats, Shakespeare was a chameleon who took equal delight in pretending to be the vile Iago and the virtuous Imogen; and Berlioz, as we'll see, is the most negatively capable of composers.

III

Berlioz's *Roméo et Juliette*

1. Berlioz in the Plural

One of the striking features of Berlioz's *Mémoires* is the indiscriminateness of his literary imagination. In 1827 *Romeo and Juliet* infused in Berlioz a dream of Italy, an ideal domain where the heaviness of the commonplace fumes away into the sheer volatility of voluptuousness; and four years later Berlioz was allowed to visit Italy—in fact compelled to live there against his will, for winners of the *Prix de Rome,* the best route to success for a young French artist, were required to live in Rome. By 1831 Italy meant to Berlioz, not amorous adventure, but the absence of amorous adventure, for his beloved (at this moment not Harriet Smithson but a woman named Camille Moke, whom Berlioz would soon come to consider calculating and unreliable) had to stay in Paris. For this reason, and for many others, including the incompetence of Italian musicians, Berlioz found Italy an exasperation and a trial. And yet Italy provided Berlioz with a huge theatre through which he could swagger, experimenting with various transvestisms between himself and dead poets, or characters in literature. He read Byron in St. Peter's, and was suddenly overwhelmed with Byron envy:

> I devoured at leisure this burning poetry; I followed the bold paths of the Corsair on the waves; I profoundly adored this character at once inexorable and tender, pitiless and generous, a bizarre composite of two sentiments seemingly opposed, hatred of his kind and love of a woman. . . . Then my thoughts, lowering their flight, took pleasure in seeking, on the basilica's pavement, the traces of the noble poet's steps. . . .
> He must have seen this sculpture by Canova, I said to myself; his feet have walked on this marble, his hands have stroked the contours of this bronze; he has breathed this air, these echoes have repeated his words . . . words of tenderness and love, perhaps. . . . Eh! yes! couldn't he have visited the monument with his friend Madame Guiccioli, that rare and admirable woman, who understood him so completely, who loved him so profoundly!!! . . . loved!!! . . . poet! . . . free! . . . rich! He was all that, himself! . . . and the grinding of my teeth, as it resounded in the confessional, would make the damned tremble with fear.[1]

In many other passages Berlioz wrapped himself in old fictitious identities:

> Sometimes, when instead of a gun I took my guitar . . . a canto of the *Aeneid,* which had been buried in my memory since childhood, awakened at the look of the places where I was wandering; improvising a strange recitative upon a still stranger harmony, I sang to myself the death of Pallas, the despair of the good Evander . . . I wept for this poor Turnus, whose land and mistress and life would be taken by the hypocrite Aeneas . . . I felt the absence of this poetic age when the heroes, sons of gods, wore such beautiful armor. . . . Leaving the past for the present, I wept for my personal griefs, my doubtful future, my interrupted career; and, collapsing overwhelmed in the midst of this chaos of poetry, murmuring some verse by Shakespeare, Virgil, and Dante: *Nessun maggior dolore . . . ô poor Ophelia . . . Good night, sweet ladies . . . sub umbras . . .* I fell asleep.[2]

> Covered (to the amusement of the Roman street urchins) with a sort of hooded cloak, similar to those that painters give to Petrarch, I accompany the cart-loads of corpses to the church across the Tiber . . . Here's a lonely village; empty except for an old woman washing her clothes in a little stream. She tells me that this silent retreat is called Isola Farnese. They say this is the modern name for the ancient Veii. This was the capital of the Volscans, those proud enemies of Rome! . . . This old woman, bent over the edge of the stream, is perhaps occupying the place where the sublime Veturia (whom Shakespeare calls Volumnia) knelt down in front of her son![3]

> The dead woman had been laid out on a table. A long dress of white percale, gathered around her neck and below her feet, covered her almost completely. Her black hair, half braided, flowed in waves around her shoulders, huge blue eyes half shut, little mouth, sad smile, neck of alabaster, noble and candid air . . . young! . . . young! . . . dead! The Italian man, always smiling, exclaimed: "*E bella!*" And, so that I could better admire her features, he lifted the head of the poor young beautiful dead girl, and, with his dirty hand, pulled apart the hair that seemed to insist, through modesty, in covering her brow and her cheeks, where there still reigned an ineffable grace. . . . I throw myself on my knees, I seize the hand of this profaned beauty, I cover her with expiatory kisses, in the throes of one of the most intense heart-anguishes of my life. . . .
>
> But suddenly I came to think: what will the husband say, if he could see the chaste hand so dear to him, recently become cold, now warmed by the kisses of young stranger? . . . would he not believe that I am the clandestine lover of his wife, who comes, more loving and more faithful than he, to breathe upon the adored body a Shakespearean despair?[4]

Berlioz in Italy lived on a stage set, in which the landscapes were painted on a scrim, so transparent that interior scenes from history and poetry kept making themselves felt through the fabric. Wisps of old presences impinge: the Countess Guiccioli seems to brush the hand of Berlioz-Byron in St. Peter's; Volumnia, disguised as a washerwoman, seems ready to bow down to Berlioz-Coriolanus; and County Paris threatens to interrupt a tender moment when Berlioz, feigning himself as the ghost of Romeo, kisses the hand of a stray Florentine Juliet. Berlioz was self-conscious in his role-playing—there are always street urchins to laugh at his Petrarch drag; but he understood his Italian sojourn as a Romantic epic improvised from scraps of old poems, hummed to a private music. Byron, Shakespeare, Virgil are all coopted, subsumed into an immense pan-literary effort.

In his private life, Berlioz toyed with a number of ultra-Romantic roles: shortly after arriving in Rome, Berlioz became alarmed at Camille Moke's unfaithfulness, and hatched a scheme to return to Paris, visit Camille disguised as a lady's maid, whip out a pistol, and shoot Camille, her lover, her mother, and at last himself—and, in case the weapon misfired, the provident assassin would have an emergency bottle of poison all ready. This scheme got as far as the purchase of the maid's costume, and a journey to the city of Nice, before Berlioz thought better and returned to Rome. Berlioz doubtlessly had many reasons for abandoning this scheme, but one reason may have been his reluctance to confine himself forever to one role, the Reckless Avenger, grotesquely appassionato, straight out of Byron's bottom drawer, when he could fantasize so many different roles for himself, could enact in his music such plurality of identity.

The heroes of Berlioz's musical compositions include King Lear, Rob Roy, Faust, Childe Harold, Benvenuto Cellini the sculptor, that hypocrite Aeneas, Romeo, Benedick (from *Much Ado about Nothing*), and the nameless artist of the *Symphonie fantastique* (1830) who takes too much opium but, instead of dying, drifts off into curious dreams of a nameless woman, modeled on Harriet Smithson. This assortment of protagonists seems extremely varied, but in fact the range of types is somewhat narrow. They can be divided into two categories: statues and sculptors. The first category consists of rigid and stolid musical subjects (such as the monothematic Childe Harold in *Harold en Italie* and Énée in *Les Troyens*), monumentally determined characters who provide a sort of dramatic tonic-note to register and orient the wild abundance that dances around them; the second category consists of the spontaneous and the improvisatory (such as Roméo and the protagonist of the *Symphonie fantastique*), those plastic sensibilities who swallow up, who *embody* the wild abundance of the whole composition. For our purposes, the second species is the important one: a hero like Berlioz's Roméo has no color or shape of his own, and only the ghost of a private voice; he is simply a sort of Aeolian harp or gramophone stylus, vibrating to various transcendental intensities of love and despair and irony. As in Wagner's *Tristan und Isolde* (1859; 1865)—a work that owes much to *Roméo et Juliette*[5]—the hero is a loud but strangely passive thing, unable to separate himself convincingly from the gorgeous web of feeling-music in which he's tangled. We tend to think of music as an expression of a human subject's states of mind; but if expression grows too big, too vehement, the human subject is drowned in the floods, and becomes a dim hypothesis, a tentative construct inferred from the simple principle that expression presupposes an expresser.

In high Romanticism, proper names tend to appear, not singly, but in effusive strings. We've seen that Hugo doesn't speak of Juliet, but of "Juliet, Desdemona, Ophelia"; and Berlioz has the same mania for whole decks of cards. In 1845, a baritone named Pischek sang at one of Berlioz's concerts in Vienna, to Berlioz's excitement: "I felt myself growing red up to my eyeballs; my arteries beat to the point of breaking, and mad with joy, I cried out, 'Voilà don Juan, voilà Roméo, voilà Cortez!'"[6] As intensity of feeling increases, specificity declines: Don Juan and Romeo and Cortez, caught at moments of lower energy, are distinct creatures; but at a point of maximum rapture all men are one man, wild with surmise.

Similarly, Berlioz's women are all one woman. When the young Berlioz wrote a cantata on an assigned text, *La mort de Cléopâtre* (1829), in order to compete for the Prix de Rome, his first thought was of Juliet:

> The subject that they gave us was Cleopatra after the battle of Actium. The queen of Egypt caused herself to be bitten by an asp, and died in convulsions. Before committing suicide, she asked the ghosts of the pharaohs . . . if she, dissolute and criminal queen, could be admitted to one of the giant tombs raised to the shades of sovereigns illustrious for glory and virtue.
>
> In this scene there was a grandiose idea to be expressed. Many times I had made in my head a musical paraphrase of the immortal monologue of Shakespeare's Juliet:
> *But if when I am laid into the tomb* . . . [4.3.30]
> The sentiment of this speech approaches, at least in its degree of terror, that of the apostrophe placed by our French rhymer in the mouth of Cleopatra. I even had the tactlessness to write as an epigraph on my score the English verse that I just quoted; and, for such Voltairean academicians as my judges, that was an unforgivable crime.[7]

(Berlioz was not given the prize, which he would receive the following year for a less challenging cantata, in which he condescended to the tastes of his judges.) The notion that music composed for a lovesick thirteen-year-old girl could be used to represent the death agony of a "dissolute and criminal queen" may suggest that Berlioz's own aesthetic of drama has a somewhat formulaic nature. In the *opere serie* of, say, Handel, arias are a fungible commodity, easily exchanged between operas: one rage aria might be transposed with another, one love aria with another. In a work by Berlioz, the principle of interchange still exists, no longer on the level of *Affekt,* but on the level of acoustic physiology. Juliet and Cleopatra approach the tomb with quite different feelings: Juliet anticipates a *mock* death as a hallucinatory ordeal—perhaps she'll go mad and "with some great kinsman's bone, / As with a club, dash out my desp'rate brain" (4.3.53–54)—an ordeal that she must undergo in order to embrace her husband; Cleopatra, by contrast is overwhelmed by despair, for she knows that she's betrayed her country and her gods, and expects the harshest judgment from the *grands Pharaons,* her ancestors. For Juliet, the tomb is a cartoon house of horrors; for Cleopatra, a complete condemnation and crushing-out of being.

But, although the emotional contents of the two scenes are quite distinct, the implied spatiality is the same. To imagine a hollow ghastly space, like the inside of a tomb, is to imagine a plangency, a plaint, equally valid for any voice that might occupy it—wicked queen or infatuated adolescent. To imagine a musical equivalent for a thready heartbeat is to imagine something appropriate for any large mammal whatsoever. At the moment of death, all differentiation falls away. Berlioz (on the evidence of his patterns of re-using melodic figures) thought that he had discovered a number of universal auditory symbols; and so a musical phrase that began in the vault of the Capulets resounded in the tomb of the Pharaohs; similarly, Berlioz borrowed the broken out-of-breath textures composed for Cleopatra's death for the funeral pyre of Dido near the end of *Les Troyens.* The careful discriminations among characters that Shakespeare and Virgil enforced, Berlioz erases. In this way Berlioz undoes characterization in the service of ecstasy, the imaginary limit-point of feeling, where Juliet and Cleopatra and Dido all converge in one terror; later we'll see how Berlioz dispenses with other aspects of drama, such as plot. Berlioz might be called a profoundly undramatic composer, in that he demands, not the steady unfolding of a story, but devastation and spasm.

Berlioz found the issue of dramatic specificity quite vexing. He poured his scorn on those Italian composers who used "conventional and invariable" musical phrases as all-purpose melodies, suitable for any text: he noted that such a composer might write a quartet in which one character was singing "O thou whom I adore," another character "What terror freezes me," a third "My heart beats with pleasure," and a fourth "Anger transports me," but neverthless "the four personages, animated by entirely opposite passions, sing successively the same melodic phrase."[8] On the other hand, Berlioz was skeptical of the referential power of music; he thought that Gluck had gone too far in instructing operatic composers to write overtures that "indicate the subject of the play":

Musical expression would not know how to go so far; it will indeed reproduce joy, sorrow, seriousness, playfulness; it will establish a striking difference between the joy of a race of shepherds and that of a nation of warriors, between the sorrow of a queen and the grief of a simple village girl, between a serious and calm meditation and the ardent reveries that precede the outbreak of passion. Moreover, by borrowing the appropriate musical style of different peoples, it will obviously be able to distinguish the serenade of a robber in the Abruzzi from that of a Tyrolian or Scottish hunter . . . it can place extreme brutality, triviality, grotesquerie, in opposition to angelic purity, nobility, and candor. But if it wishes to escape from this large circle, music must necessarily resort to the word, sung, recited, or read, to fill the gaps that its means of expression leave . . . Thus the overture to [Gluck's] *Alceste* announces scenes of desolation and tenderness, but it does not know how to speak either the object of the tenderness or the causes of this desolation. . . .[9]

Berlioz goes on to speculate that his readers may be surprised that he (the arch-expressive) has such a narrow view of the possibilities of musical expression. A little later in his essay on *Alceste,* Berlioz returns to the problem of vagueness and particularity in music theatre; he rehearses a scene in which Gluck's chorus, told "Your king is going to die!," flees in panic:

J. J. Rousseau reproached this *allegro agitato* for expressing equally well the disorderliness of joy as that of terror. One can respond that the composer found himself, at that moment, at the limit or meeting-point of two passions, and that it was consequently almost impossible not to incur such a reproach. The proof lies in the fact that, hearing the vociferations of a crowd rushing from one place to another, the listener placed at a distance would not know how to discover whether the sentiment that agitates the crowd is fear or mad gaiety. . . . A composer can easily write a chorus whose joyous intention would never be misunderstood, but the reverse isn't true; and the agitations of a[n unhappy] crowd translated into music, when those agitations are not caused by hate or the desire for vengeance, will greatly resemble . . . tumultuous joy.[10]

Berlioz thought that a skillful composer could take advantage of the frailty of musical semantics, by writing music in which ambiguity of meaning could be a form of power. Coleridge liked oxymorons because they represented a potent state of hovering between images; Gluck (as Berlioz heard him) composed a musical oxymoron, equivocating tensely between disorderly joy and disorderly terror. Berlioz defended this on the grounds of realism (a far-off listener wouldn't know the feeling that provoked the crowd's noise); but he also is appealing to a theory of convergence—at the peak of intensity, all feelings meet. On the lower levels of sensation, a queen feels a quality of pain distinct from that of a shepherdess; a Scottish reel can be differentiated from a tarantella through characteristic habits of rhythm. But Berlioz seemed to find these discriminations slightly crude, and seemed somewhat impatient to rush into realms of musical expression where systems of signs first grow giddy, then collapse.

Berlioz's rule seems to be this: music sinks into recitation in order to make dramatic conflicts clear; then music soars into its private sky in order to supersede those conflicts.

2. *Roméo et Juliette*: Introduction and Prologue

When Berlioz came to write *Roméo et Juliette,* he therefore faced a twin problem: first, to tell an exciting story; second, to untell the story, to move into a region beyond narrative and drama. He read Shakespeare's play (in French translation, and haltingly in the original) in order to seek clues for achieving the peculiar dramatic rhythm he sought; and he may have pondered a number of operas on the Romeo and Juliet theme, by Daniel Steibelt (1793), Nicolas-Marie Dalayrac (1792), Niccolò Zingarelli (1796), Nicola Vaccai (1825), and, of course, Bellini (1830). (We know that Berlioz had heard Bellini's opera by 1831; he mentioned the other operas in a feuilleton of 1859, and it isn't certain that he knew them before writing his own *Roméo et Juliette.*) He found little to please him in any of these works, grumbling at the general absence of Mercutio, the Nurse, and Rosaline—all the jejune or grotesque peripheral characters who were to Berlioz (as to Hugo) the hallmarks of Shakespeare's art. Furthermore, he detested the decision, by all three Italian composers, to assign the role of Romeo to a female voice:

> It's the result of a constant preoccupation with sensual infantilism. They wanted women to sing the role of male lovers, because in duet the two feminine voices more easily produce chains of thirds, dear to the Italian ear. . . . low voices horrified this public of sybarites, fond of sonorous sweetness as children are fond of candy.[11]

Berlioz preferred an explicit contrast of gender—though a partisan of Bellini might point out, first, that Shakespeare's own theatre had a Romeo and Juliet of the same gender, and second, that the Romeo of Bellini and his librettist, Felice Romani, is a far more masculine and warlike character than Shakespeare's—Romani's Romeo is an experienced commander of troops who plans to snatch Juliet by force of arms from the bosom of the Capulets. In any case, when Berlioz came to write his own version of the tale, he dispensed with human voices entirely for the roles of Romeo and Juliet, allowed them to be portrayed by orchestral instruments that could assume different registers or the same register, and thereby heightening or flattening the contrast between the lovers at the composer's pleasure. Sometimes Berlioz's Romeo and Juliet are highly gendered creatures; at other times they slough off the signs of sexual identity, ascend into a bodiless elysium of love.

There was one moment in Bellini's opera that Berlioz found full of *élan*: a unison phrase for Romeo and Juliet in the finale to the first act:

> The two lovers were forcibly separated by their furious parents; the Montagues held Romeo, the Capulets Juliet; but at the last return of the beautiful phrase "We will meet in heaven!" they both escaped from the hands of their persecutors, and threw themselves into one another's arms and embraced with a completely Shakespearean furor. At that moment one began to believe in their love.[12]

Berlioz complained that duets in the unison became commonplace after Bellini's example; but in 1831, when he saw the opera, such a procedure seemed original and salient. The unison phrase *Se ogni speme è a noi rapita* is indeed remarkable, a passage of rapid sinuous despair that seems to inhabit a different plane of music from the bellicose massed voices on either side; it is also, in its unexpected twists, an extraordinarily Berlioz-like melody. Perhaps here Berlioz found part of the central premise of *Roméo et Juliette,* the notion that love music could be embedded inside war music and yet remain inviolate, immiscible, speaking a private language in the midst of public conflict.

Berlioz married his Juliet in 1833—"Henriette Smithson, being ruined and scarcely healed [from her broken leg], I married her, despite the violent opposition of her family."[13] The marriage turned out to be unhappy, and Berlioz's decision to write *Roméo and Juliette* (1839) may be seen as his attempt to recover the only Juliet he could ever truly possess, the Juliet of his imagination.

The obvious way of treating the Romeo and Juliet theme was to write an opera. There was a biographical reason that tended to inhibit Berlioz from doing so: his enemies could prevent him from producing a new work in the only theatre in France that could properly mount an opera. But there was also a technical reason for Berlioz's decision to treat the theme in a non-operatic fashion: he wanted to transcend the limitations of operatic theatre, with its often fallible and coarse singers, its rigid body of absurdly predictable conventions. Late in his life Berlioz met a fan of *Roméo et Juliette,* who demanded that Berlioz write an opera on the same theme: Berlioz replied,

> Alas, monsieur . . . where are two artists capable of singing and playing the two principal roles? They do not exist; and, if they did exist, thanks

to the musical customs and usages that prevail in every lyric theatre, if I put such an opera into rehearsal, I would be sure to die before the first performance.[14]

The fan responded, "Let Berlioz die! but let him do it!" But Berlioz felt he had done the right thing by emancipating *Roméo et Juliette* from the vagaries and *niaiseries* of the opera house: as he wrote in the preface to the score,

> the duets of love and despair are entrusted to the orchestra . . . [since] duets of this nature have been treated vocally a thousand times by the greatest masters, it was prudent as well as novel [*curieux*] to attempt another mode of expression . . . [and] because the very sublimity of this love made its depiction so dangerous for the composer that he had to give to his fantasy a latitude that the definite meaning [*sens positif*] of sung words would never have allowed him.[15]

In order to be worthy of Shakespeare, Berlioz felt that he needed to write a work that undid opera, a sort of anti-opera.

Roméo et Juliette became one of the most generically challenging works of the nineteenth century. What is the genre of a piece that begins with a choral exposition of the subject matter, complete with a tenor singing about Queen Mab; then embarks on a full-scale symphony, in which each movement has a Shakespearean gloss; and at last ends with an extensive and expensive operatic scene, in which Friar Lawrence confronts and cows the massed Capulets and Montagues? The *Symphonie dramatique* is a mixture of many sorts of genres—symphony, cantata, oratorio, opera, operetta, even art song (the Strophes in Part One were originally composed for voice and guitar[16]). The oratorio, in Berlioz's time, had particular importance as a site for research into the blurring of genre. Berlioz's teacher Le Sueur wrote four experimental "mass-oratorios" (1786–87) for Christmas, Easter, Pentecost, and the Assumption; and *Roméo et Juliette* can be understood as a secular equivalent of these, a hybrid between an abstract celebration of the god of love and a theatrical enactment of love's ritual.

Roméo et Juliette aspires to go beyond finite genres through the act of comprehending all at once. In this sense its analogue in the domain of literature is the novel—for the Romantic imagination, the novel was a sort of *Über*-genre, breaking down the boundaries between various types of literature.[17] Goethe's *Wilhelm Meister,* for example, is a novel that concerns (among many other things) a disreputable theatre company and a strolling harper—a novel that may be said to include dramas inside itself, as well as dramatic criticism, and some of the most haunting lyric poems in the German language, as if the text were an open field for any sort of discourse whatever. Similarly, *Roméo et Juliette* owes its bulging form to the fact that it is a symphony that has swallowed an opera—the opera keeps spilling out around the edges. For Berlioz as for Mahler, the symphony is cosmic in scale, incomplete if there's any sort of music that it doesn't contain; the symphony can only realize itself by trying to comprehend what is usually considered non-symphonic.

There is, of course, a famous precedent for a symphony that ends with a big movement for chorus and soloists: the Ninth Symphony of Beethoven (1824), in which Schiller's Ode to Joy becomes a basis for a sort of interplanetary rejoicing in music. Beethoven was the only musician known to Berlioz who seemed to have something of Shakespeare's comprehensive grasp of human life; and Berlioz was one of the few musicians living in the years after Beethoven's death in 1827 who was in a position to confront the Ninth Symphony and to attempt to compose an even more ambitious work along similar lines. Indeed the circumstances of the composition of *Roméo et Juliette* also seemed to invite a challenge to resurrect Beethoven: the work was funded by the wealthy violinist Paganini—Berlioz had little money and many enemies, since he was a music critic as well as a composer; after hearing a concert of Berlioz's music in 1838, Paganini offered Berlioz 20,000 francs, together with a note saying that, "since Beethoven is dead, only Berlioz can make him live again."[18] (As David B. Levy has shown,[19] even in Germany, some important music critics, such as Wolfgang Robert Griepenkerl, agreed with Paganini that Berlioz was the rightful heir to Beethoven.) There is no better introduction to Berlioz's *Roméo et Juliette* than Beethoven's Ninth.

But Berlioz was accustomed to hearing *all* of Beethoven's symphonies—not just the Ninth—as musical embodiments of literary masterpieces, as if every movement in Beethoven had an occult programmatic content. To listen to the adagio of Beethoven's Fourth is to sob as Virgil sobbed when hearing the "touching story of Francesca da Rimini" in Dante's *Inferno*;[20] as for the first movement of the Fifth Symphony, it is

a depiction of disordered feelings that overwhelm a great soul prey to despair; not the concentrated, calm despair that has the look of resignation; not the black mute pain of Romeo learning of Juliet's death, but indeed the terrible rage of Othello, receiving from Iago's mouth the poisonous slanders that persuade him of Desdemona's crime.[21]

The Allegretto of Beethoven's Seventh—the best-loved symphonic movement in France, in Berlioz's time—contains a melody (as Berlioz described it) "sad and resigned *like patience smiling at grief*" (*Twelfth Night* 2.4.114–15) and ends with "the wind instruments exhaling a deep sigh on an indecisive harmony and . . . *the rest is silence*" (*Hamlet* 5.2.358).[22] It is as if Beethoven's music were not only rehearsing stories from Shakespeare and Dante, but even trying to utter certain particularly telling lines from these classic poets. The more Berlioz could become Beethoven, the more he would succeed in being Shakespeare: for Beethoven's symphonies sounded like Shakespeare's rhetoric, liberated from Shakespeare's text. Beethoven had written an Othello symphony, but hadn't made his theme explicit; Berlioz would write a Romeo and Juliet symphony, in such a way that everyone would know it.

Berlioz went to considerable trouble to try to articulate as clearly as possible the structure of the work—no easy task, for it was composed in defiance of normal music structures. Berlioz's plan of the work[23] illustrates that *Roméo et Juliette* is, despite all its incrustations and complexifications, a genuine symphony:

1. *Introduction: Combats—Tumulte—Intervention du Prince*
   (Introduction: Combats—Tumult—Intervention by the Prince)
   Prologue
   Strophes
   Scherzetto
2. *Roméo seul—Tristesse—Bruits lointains de bal et de concert—
   Grande Fête chez Capulet* (Romeo alone—Sadness—Faraway
   noises of the ball and the concert—Great festival at the Capulets')
3. *Nuit sereine—Le Jardin de Capulet, silencieux et désert* (Serene
   Night—Capulet's garden, silent and deserted)
   Scène d'amour (Love Scene)
4. *La Reine Mab, ou la Fée des Songes: Scherzo* (Queen Mab, or the
   fairy of dreams: Scherzo)
5. *Convoi funèbre de Juliette* (Juliet's funeral procession)
6. *Roméo au tombeau des Capulets* (Romeo at the tomb of the
   Capulets)
   Invocation
7. *Final*
   Air
   Serment

At the first performance (but deleted afterward) there was also a second choral prologue, just before Juliet's Funeral Procession, explaining that Juliet was dead (or seemed to be), and otherwise making audible the plot line of the final episodes; an intermission preceded the second prologue.

This is a truly bizarre plan for a musical composition. Sections 2, 3, and 4 correspond pretty clearly to the first three movements of a standard symphony: a movement developing two themes (equivalent to a sonata form movement), a slow movement, and a scherzo; but section 1 provides far too much prefatory material, and sections 5, 6, and 7 drift off into regions difficult to construe as appropriate to a symphony. The most obvious oddity is the amount of space occupied by Queen Mab; but the role of the chorus is even stranger. At the beginning, the chorus is a talking program note, but by the final scene the chorus is joining into the larger chorus that plays the crowd of Montagues and Capulets. The small chorus of the Prologue has to teach the larger chorus of the finale the role it will play; we are uncomfortably close to the world of Peter Quince and the hempen homespuns in *A Midsummer Night's Dream,* who first discuss and rehearse the Pyramus and Thisby skit, and then play it. Berlioz's chorus, unlike Peter Quince's gang, will not break character in the midst of the finale to tell the audience not to get too upset by the general ickiness of the tragedy; but a chorus (if we consider it as a single entity) that has first commented upon the Montagues and Capulets, and then assumed the roles, will not go far toward suspending the audience's disbelief. The finale is a walloping operatic scene, but a scene in quotation marks: the chorus has simply pursued the goal of *explication* by other means. The work ends—as Shakespeare's own play ends—with a combination of tragedy and narrative: a huge loud gloss on itself.

Berlioz was a music critic, and his chorus has an essentially critical temperament, patiently analyzing the structure, highlighting the principal themes of the music in which it takes part. If Berlioz had incorporated his own analytical commentary into Beethoven's Fifth Symphony—"and now, ladies and gentlemen, Iago whispers in Othello's ear; hear Othello *roar*"—by means of choral interjections, and then allowed the chorus to impersonate Lodovico and Montano and the other worthies at the end of the symphony, caught up in a blaze of revelation, Berlioz might have made Beethoven's work a *dramatic* symphony. But the germ of the notion of a symphony that incorporates a kind of music criticism of itself may be derived from Beethoven, for the first words heard in the Ninth Symphony are "O friends, not these sounds"—as if the bass soloist were a stray music critic who interrupted the dissonant tumult in the finale in order to make a public gesture of clapping his hands over his ears, to encourage the musicians to play something more soothing.[24]

It is highly appropriate that Berlioz made his chorus so eager to provide plot summary, explanation, and description, for the chorus—indeed the whole operatic part of the symphony—represents the public, honor-driven world of Shakespeare's Verona. What is the musical equivalent of the social code? A music that is nice in its precisions, self-critical, polished. The music of the social code is music that a critic would applaud: attentive to old formalities of composition. Disobedience is so central to Berlioz's Romanticism that the operatic parts of *Roméo et Juliette* show a great many original and striking features; but whether conventional or unconventional, the operatic parts are *about* music, extremely self-conscious about technique and form. The symphony (sections 2, 3, and 4) yearns toward unconsciousness, toward direct incarnation of feeling; but the opera (sections 1, 5, 6, and 7) scrutinizes its own musical devices.

Example 1. Fugue-War

What sort of music would have seemed, in France in the 1830s, an appropriate image of the social code—stiff, formal, legislated? Arguably, a fugue. Here perhaps, if anywhere, is music for music's sake: a fugue may suggest an intellectual artifice that holds itself above the mess of human expression; it may suggest religious austerity, a clockwork precision of control. Berlioz's *Roméo et Juliette* begins with exactly this, a fugue—but a fugue so hectic and erratic, so hard to follow, that it becomes an image, not of calm obedience to a set of instructions, not of Friar Lawrence's heavenward glance, but of the general havoc of the life of the Montagues and Capulets (see example 1). From the first bar of his dramatic symphony, Berlioz illustrates the untenability of the Veronese social code: it has generated into an incomprehensible fury of bristling voices. We begin with a vendetta in music, the "new mutiny / Where civil blood makes civil hands unclean," as Shakespeare puts it in *his* prologue.

But soon the frenzy abates, and the texture thins to a single line, as the brass utters a slow incontrovertible theme, establishing a sort of authority over the orchestral chaos (see example 2). This section of the score is marked *Fieramente, un poco ritenuto, col carattere di Recitativo, misurato* [Fiercely, a little held back, with the character of a recitative, measured]: it is Prince Escalus quashing, almost squashing, the quarrel, as Berlioz performs an astonishing stunt of making instrumental music do the work of speaking words—the brass intones lines obviously corresponding to Shakespeare's "Rebellious subjects, enemies to peace . . . If ever you disturb the streets

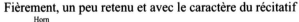

Example 2. Prince Escalus intervenes

again / Your lives shall pay the forfeit of the peace" (1.1.81, 96–97). Harmonically, Escalus inhabits a completely different plane from that of the disputants: whereas the fugue picked itself apart in B minor, the solemn warning begins in B♭ major, a very remote key; but melodically, Escalus is himself one of the Veronese, for he sings *the very same tune* as that of the fugue, immensely slowed down and clarified. Berlioz's extraordinary subtlety with systems of signs is already evident: Escalus is dramatically differentiated from the Capulets and Montagues, but in such a way that he is assimilated, in occult fashion, into the very feud above which he tries to stand. Escalus's law code isn't the same as the vendetta code of the Montagues and Capulets; and yet Escalus is part of the same domain of paternal governance as the Montagues and Capulets, the domain that Romeo and Juliet must learn to defy.

After this brief orchestral Introduction comes the Prologue, for chorus and contralto and tenor soloists. (Berlioz wrote a prose version of the libretto—if such a brief, sketchy, and incoherent collection of synopsis, metapoetic effusion, and grand-opera finale can be called a libretto—which was then versified by his friend Émile Deschamps.[25]) The orchestral Introduction was bewilderingly eventful; but in the subsequent choral recitative the density of events slows down almost to zero. As the chorus explains what the listener has already heard—that two old families are at war, and that the prince has threatened them with death—it sings in a spare chordal texture, with little melodic or harmonic motion, in a manner only slightly more musical than plain spoken narrative. But as the chorus starts to anticipate the rest of plot—Romeo stands outside the palace of the Capulets, weeping, for he loves the daughter of his family's enemies, and he sees the shine of gold and hears the melodious sounds of the dance—suddenly the recitative is interrupted by the orchestra, playing the music of the Capulets' ball, just as we will hear it in the first symphonic movement of Part Two. The Prologue is turning into a *thematic catalogue*, for *Roméo et Juliette* is a symphony that incorporates its own playbill. Berlioz is instructing us how to interpret the purely instrumental music to come—it is as if *Roméo et Juliette* begins with the Cliff's Notes to itself, a set of cues to its semantic organization. (In the fine phrase of Jacques Chailley, the Prologue "constitutes a veritable *musical analysis of the score, inserted into the score itself.*"[26]) This is how Berlioz avoids what might be called the Gluck problem: the inability of an overture to confess much about the drama to come. Berlioz writes a talking "overture," a Prologue in which the composer stands at the blackboard, pointer in hand, and lectures to the audience. It is an audacious and curiously intimate strategy, as if the musician gives us a tour of his workshop before we begin the difficult task of hearing the work.

In this way, Berlioz creates an evacuated musical space on which explication can be inscribed. But as the choral recitative continues, the impetuous professor starts to scribble his analysis more quickly. The chorus sings chant the program notes, then sing a very simple strophic song about ah, young love, then finally deliver a delectable *drolerie*.

The tenor cannot be identified too closely with Mercutio himself, since he sings the speech-prefix (*dit l'élégant Mercutio*) as well as the text of the speech. The tenor *quotes* the song; we are approximating the mode of drama, but not yet within it—the scherzetto, like everything else in the Prologue, is still in the critical-analytic mode. Note that Mercutio's speech about "Mab, the light and slender messenger"—*Mab, la messagère / Fluette et légère*—is echoed by the chorus, in a way familiar to Anglophone audiences from such later roles as Captain Corcoran in Sullivan's *H. M. S. Pinafore* ("And never, never sick at sea. *Chorus*: What, never?"): the tenor who half-impersonates Mercutio is a patter-song specialist, a vaudevillean like Maurice Chevalier, tilting his hat and twinkling at the audience, delivering his star-turn with practiced charm. This isn't to say that the music is unsophisticated: far from it, for the accompaniment figure keeps overreaching, spanning a minor ninth, from C to D♭—that D♭, borrowed from the F minor scale, remains a sort of unassimilable eccentricity in the key of F major, as if to symbolize the fact that the settled pseudo-operatic world of the frame is yielding to the unstable, dazzlingly new musical universe of the love symphony.

The scherzetto doesn't cite music from the scherzo to come, but it anticipates its airy texture, its controlled simulation of loss of control: the Prologue concludes with music that lifts and lightens, dissolves; after the lecturer has written down all his messages, he erases the blackboard, for we are half to remember, half to forget, the instruction of the Introduction and Prologue. At the end of the scherzetto, a cock crows, and we wake up, only to fall under the spell of a different hypnosis. When the symphony proper begins, we listen with cleansed ears: we are left, not with a dry musicological treatise, but with a set of subliminal expectations, nudging the mind into the channels of interpretation that Berlioz intended. And the scherzetto also provides a good lead-in to what follows, in that its key is very remote from the B minor of the Introduction—in fact its F major will turn out to be the home key of the symphony. The harmonic evolution of section 1 has spanned a tritone. Queen Mab herself is *diabola in musica,* a succubus, a nightmare; and so she belongs out-of-phase, harmonically speaking, from the common life of Verona.

3. *Roméo et Juliette*: The Symphony

Now we begin the symphony proper, with a long movement called *Roméo seul* that, like many first movements of symphonies in the tradition of Haydn and Mozart and Beethoven, starts with a slow introduction, *Andante*

Example 4. Roméo in solitude

malinconico e sostenuto. But the theme of introduction is untraditional: an immensely long line, sparsely accompanied, not so much an intelligible melody as a pitch-contour suitable for shading and expressive shaping—a sort of naked expressivity purged of easily interpreted expressive devices, a *stile molle* not quite certain exactly what form of melancholy it wants to take. It is difficult to grasp the form of the whole line, difficult even to grasp the key: sometimes it seems to present itself in F major (appropriate to the single-flat signature), but it seems equally at home in C major and A minor, and has distinct sociopathic tendencies to the remote key of E major. It is a juvenile-delinquent melody, sullen, tentative, rebellious, unpredictable. Although its direction keeps wavering, the listener soon grows accustomed to a half-articulate pattern of a leap, a sustained note, and, trailing off the sustained note, an irregular chromatic droop. It is a tune without a *Gestalt,* persistently unsuitable to symphonic development. Or, to put it another way, it can't be developed precisely because it keeps developing itself, as segments of itself keep looping back to other keys. Symphonic development is largely a matter of extracting pieces of a theme, and subjecting those pieces to sequential treatment; but in a long, auto-sequencing theme, such as Berlioz's introduction to *Roméo seul* (or the *idée fixe* of the *Symphonie fantastique*), it is impossible to distinguish exposition from development (example 4).[28]

Why would Berlioz want to begin the symphonic part of his *Roméo et Juliette* in such a state of musical obscurity? One reason is that it is evidently evening, and the thick dimness of the music, as it gropes for a theme, reflects the time of day. But another reason is that, for Berlioz, vagueness is power. In 1832, Berlioz wrote that Weber and Beethoven had invented a new sort of music, the *genre instrumental expressif*:

> In former times instrumental music seems to have had no other aim than to please the ear or to engage the intellect . . . but in Beethoven's and Weber's works, one cannot miss the poetic thought . . . It is music which gives way to itself, needing no words to make its expression spe-

Réunion des deux Thèmes, du Larghetto et de l'Allegro

Example 5. Ball music in treble clef, *Larghetto* in accented notes in bass clef

human voices are subsumed into regions of greater expressive intensity, the blaze of the orchestra, so any mimetic music must be subsumed into a larger frame of sonority. Just as joy and terror may be utterly conjoint and confounded in a single musical work, so Romeo's solitude and the Capulets' blatancy may be pulled together into one knot of dark thick expressivity.

Roméo seul was not Berlioz's first experiment with the A B A/B structure—his private alternative to sonata form. The rondo of the Witches' Sabbath, the fifth movement of the *Symphonie fantastique,* is designed in the same way: two themes, the *Dies irae* and a ghastly dance tune, are first separately stated and finally superimposed. A similar, more casual phenomenon may be found in the Pilgrims' March in *Harold en Italie* (1834), where the processional theme wends through the interstices of Harold's inflexible theme, as if it filed its way, not through a mountain landscape, but through the inside of Harold's brain. The precedent of *Harold en Italie* is important, for it suggested the psychologizing potential of the method: exterior, mimetic music could be audibly assimilated into the mind of the protagonist, simply by allowing the protagonist to keep a grip on the rhythm, the melos, of the inner workings of his consciousness, at the same time that his ears are hearing some foreign sound.

Where might Berlioz have discovered a prototype for this odd sort of development by addition? One clue is found in the *Mémoires,* in Berlioz's account of the rowdy behavior of his fellow students in Rome:

> We had a type of concert that we called *English concerts* . . . The drinkers, more or less capable of singing, each with his favorite song, prepared to sing as many different tunes as possible; moreover, to get the greatest variety, each sang in a key different from that of the man next to

him. Duc, the witty, wise architect, sang his song of *La Colonne,* Dantan
that of *Sultan Saladin,* Monfort triumphed in the march of *La Vestale .
. .* and I had some success with the air, so tender and naive, *Il pleut
bergère.* At a given signal, the participants set out one after another, and
this vast ensemble in twenty-four parts was performed in a crescendo,
accompanied by the sad howls of frightened dogs. . . .[30]

But of course the superimpository technique of *Roméo seul* isn't comic, in
the fashion of Biber or the students' *English concert.* Besides the comic
overlay of the *English concert,* there is also, in the musical world of Berlioz's
time, a species of tragic overlay. This is to be found, not in symphonic
music, but in an advanced operatic technique. I'll illustrate this with two
examples, both from operas extremely familiar to Berlioz.

Spontini's *La Vestale* (1807) takes place in ancient Rome. A young noble-
woman, Julia, loves Licinius, a commoner, who despairs of marrying her;
he joins the army in order to win glory and become worthy. But during his
absence Julia's father dies, committing her to become a vestal virgin, forever sworn to chastity. Licinius returns from war, a victorious general, adored
by the whole of Rome; but Julia is torn between her desperate desire to see
him and her will to be faithful to her vow to Vesta. In the fifth scene of the
first act, Julia hears the approach of Licinius in triumph—a light, sparky
march (the very march mentioned in Berlioz's story of the English concert)
sung by a chorus of warriors; but she feels pain, not joy, and over the
march soars her vocal line, *Ô trouble . . . ô terreur . . . L'effroi . . . glace
mon coeur!* The fear that ices her heart is expressed by music that utterly
contradicts the march tune beneath: the broken text is sung to a shattered,
shrieky sort of melody. Julia and the chorus—psychology and publicity—
inhabit separate musical spaces, forcibly conjoined by the overlay technique.

Cherubini's *Médée* (1797) concerns the notorious sorceress of Greek
myth, who murdered her children in order to punish their father, the argo-
naut Jason, for his faithlessness. The finale of the second act provides one
of the subtlest, most complex applications of overlay technique ever written: it is basically a long processional hymn to celebrate the wedding of
Jason and Dircé; but the scene is dominated by a non-participant, Medea,
who watches the festivities in a state of acute rage. The music for the ceremony is slightly scored, tripping, gay—in places drowned out by the superimposed voice (spoken, not sung) of Medea, cursing the happy pair,
cackling over her wedding gift to Dircé, a poisoned diadem. What is remarkable is the role of the orchestra: at the beginning, it's fully devoted to
the joy of the procession, and pays only brief attention to the exclamations
of Medea. The chorus ignores her entirely—she's out of their earshot, rapt
in soliloquy—but from time to time Medea succeeds in destabilizing the
orchestra, bending it to her fury: when she screams a curse during the cho-

ral invocation of Hymen, the orchestra sends up a dark ejaculation from its depths, full of chromatic tremoli, before remembering that its duty is to accompany the songs of love. Throughout the scene, Medea and the chorus compete for the orchestra's attention: the orchestra keeps negotiating the divide between obedient support for a hymn, and psychotic expressivity. The depth of the musical-dramatic field is remarkable, as the orchestra continually adjusts its focus from foreground to background. In the final section, as the chorus reaches its climax, begging the son of Bacchus to fulfill the vows of the married couple, the tremoli associated with Medea's rage start to infect the hymn-tune, and Medea at last begins to sing: she makes a counter-address to Hymen, trying to deflect the choral plea for joy into a plea for vengeance; and she succeeds, insofar as the whole orchestral texture swerves into a depiction of her rage. The orchestra itself is like the god whom Medea and the chorus invoke, giving itself to the party whose emotional intensity is the greatest.

Cherubini is one of the villains of Berlioz's *Mémoires,* the director of the Conservatoire during the time of Berlioz's study, a dragon of orthodoxy. But some of Berlioz's greatest achievements draw strongly on the work of Cherubini—especially, I think, when Berlioz wanted to construct multi-planar musical entities. Cherubini had sophisticated lessons to offer, concerning the simultaneous presentation of public music and private music, tragically incommensurate. At the end of the first act of *Les Troyens* (1858), Berlioz followed the example of Cherubini's *Medée* with extreme accuracy: the Trojans, impressed by the generosity of the Greeks, are bringing the enormous wooden horse through the city gates, to the festive strains of the Trojan march and hymn (eventually infected by a queasy lower counterpoint), while at the same time the overwrought Cassandre prophesies the ruin of Troy, to very different music. The chorus ignores the famously ignored seeress, but the orchestra turns toward her an anxious ear. A little less than twenty years earlier, in *Roméo seul,* Berlioz found a way of adapting this sort of operatic discourse to a symphonic discourse in which the orchestra assimilated all the voices, the public voice, the private voice, the accompanying commentary to these two voices, into its own plasticity.

In the examples from Cherubini and Spontini and *Les Troyens,* the lower plane is public and choral; the solo vocal line is plunked on top of a ceremonious mass. But in *Roméo seul* Berlioz turns this procedure upside down. Here the first music, the fundamental music, is the Larghetto, the theme of Romeo's solitude; the evocation of the ball in the allegro section is the intruder, the more extrinsic element. This is true even on the level of pitch: in the *Réunion des deux Thèmes* section, the larghetto theme is (relative to the ball music) a lower, more basic voice, conspicuous in the trombones, to which the ball music must accommodate itself—in the continuation, Berlioz even alters a few details of pitch in the allegro theme to adjust it to the larghetto theme. (These themes were clearly devised to facilitate combination; but the ball music seems to respect the governing power of the larghetto theme.) The charged individual intelligence has primacy; as for the public world, the more deeply we enter into the symphonic portion of *Roméo et Juliette,* the more vain, the more wraith-like, it becomes. The mind of Romeo eats up the Capulets' ball; and in the *Réunion* we hear what a festivity sounds like, after a listener has digested it. Romeo Romeizes the static cheer of the ballroom music, parcels it out into the interspaces of his own theme. His intense solitude triumphs.

The formal procedures in *Roméo seul* are self-conscious, even willful: Berlioz makes the listener aware of scissors and glue-pot, as he pastes one theme on top of another and *labels* them to make his process explicit. Its cleverness of shape may even seem slightly distasteful, as if Berlioz were performing a stunt or proving a thesis, instead of allowing his music to develop in any easy manner. But when we come to the next movement, the Adagio (in A major, the mediant of F), we abandon conscious contrivance and enter a simulation of unconscious desire, groping for expression.

Berlioz agreed with the discerning critics who considered this movement his highest achievement as a composer,[31] and it was certainly embedded in his erotic sensibility: in 1847, in St. Petersburg, Berlioz seduced a young corset-maker by crushing her arm to his breast and singing in her ear "the beautiful phrase of the adagio of *Roméo et Juliette.*"[32] The adagio has also seduced a number of Berlioz's critics, who have scrutinized it with the care it deserves. D. Kern Holoman has vividly described the essentially strophic nature of this huge movement,[33] and it is indeed a song, around twenty minutes in length, emancipated from the constraint of words, the constraint of the singer's breath supply, the constraint of any form beyond the organic form it generates through its own immense evolution.

Near the beginning we hear the chorus, impersonating the happy and exhausted revelers from the Capulets' festival, tra-la-la-ing their way home. This is the only appearance of actual human voices in the three symphonic movements of *Roméo et Juliette*; and I suspect that Berlioz added the choral part in order to make an audible image of vanishing: human voices are slowly extinguished, in order to make space for the superhuman voices of Romeo and Juliet, in a sealed, self-engrossed world. In *Roméo seul,* the festival is loudly incorporated into Romeo's reverie; in the Adagio, the festival tapers to nothingness, so that we may enter the nirvana of love. In the first movement the antithesis between the private and the public is strong; in the second movement, it is overcome, ravished away, at least for a while, by the simple means of deleting one of its terms.

After the chorus dispells itself, and the adagio proper begins, the orchestra first plays bird calls, cicada chirrups—serene twitters and cooings in the night. These sounds are a source of vexation for critics. Where, in Shakespeare's text, do we find birds?—not in the balcony scene (except for a simile involving falcons), but much later, in the post-coital scene, which is a meditation on the identity of bird calls:

> *Jul.* Wilt thou be gone? it is not yet near day,
> It was the nightingale, and not the lark,
> That pierc'd the fearful hollow of thine ear;
> Nightly she sings on yond pomegranate tree.
> Believe me, love, it was the nightingale.
> *Rom.* It was the lark, the herald of the morn,
> No nightingale. (3.5.1–7)

This is the most obviously operatic passage in the whole play—as we know from Gounod, and Tchaikovsky, who set a Russian translation of this passage to the love music in his *Romeo and Juliet* fantasy-overture, in a sketch for an unwritten opera (Taneyev's completion of this scene was first performed in 1894).

But neither nightingale nor lark has any obvious business in the balcony scene; and Berlioz's program is clear that the adagio represents first Romeo in the Capulets' orchard, then Romeo and Juliet in the balcony scene. Now, it is certainly plausible that an orchard at night might be adorned with bird calls, even if Shakespeare didn't have much to say about them; but Berlioz's music has teased listeners, from the very first performances, into thinking of the nightingales and larks in Shakespeare's third act. Julian Rushton, in his superbly detailed handbook on *Roméo et Juliette,* cites a newspaper critic from 1839 who referred to lark and nightingale[34] in connection with the music at the end of the adagio; Rushton, eager to keep Berlioz's adagio within the confines of the balcony scene, contradicts the critic, but perhaps there's an argument to be made in favor of the ornithologist who wishes to hear, not just at the end, but throughout the adagio, confused echoes of the nightingale that pierces the fearful hollow of the ear.

Shakespeare's play as it existed in Berlioz's memory differs strongly from Shakespeare's play as it exists on the page. Indeed many aspects of Berlioz's dramatic symphony may be described as creative misrememberings of Shakespeare. In his essay of 1859 on musical settings of *Romeo and Juliet* (not including his own), Berlioz summarizes Shakespeare's balcony scene as follows:

> And after the festival, wandering around Capulet's house, prey to a divine anguish, beginning to feel the immense revolution going on inside him, he hears the avowal of the noble girl, he trembles with astonishment and joy; and then begins the immortal dialogue worthy of the angels of heaven: [Berlioz cites the passage beginning with Juliet's "I gave thee mine before thou didst request it"].
>
> But Romeo must leave, and his heart feels the grip of an intense pain, and he says to his beloved: "I cannot conceive that they can separate us,

I can scarcely understand that I must leave you, even if for only a few hours. Listen, among these harmonies that burst out from afar, for this rising long cry of pain. . . . It seems to come out of my breast. . . . Look at these splendors of heaven, look at all these brilliant lights, would you not say that the fairies have lit up their palaces to celebrate our love? . . ." And Juliet, trembling, answers only with tears. And a true great love is born, immense, inexplicable, armed with every power of the imagination, the heart, and the senses.[35]

Berlioz evidently wrote this passage with a French translation of Shakespeare on his desk, since he quotes accurately from the balcony scene. And yet the passage that appears in quotation marks, beginning "I cannot conceive," is a pure hallucination, without basis in Shakespeare's text. Garrick's text has no such speech, either; and I find it difficult to believe that any adaptation of Shakespeare's text would include such a thing, for there is no Shakespearean scene in which it would be appropriate—"harmonies that burst out from afar" seem appropriate only to the virtual theatre of Berlioz's imagination. This speech is a vocalizing of Berlioz's own subvocal music, in which the balcony scene is reconceived symphonically, in terms of sonorous spaces, distant harmonies of the revelers, a crescendo of pain from the solitary lover, even a faint sprinkle of Queen Mab's fairy music descending from the sky. The whole play, as reimagined by Berlioz, is brought to bear on this strange literary paraphrase of the balcony scene.

And I believe that, when Berlioz wrote the Adagio, the whole play was also brought to bear on the love scene. This wordless duet is simultaneously the chaste avowal in the balcony scene and the carnal embrace in the third act; it is not any single love duet, but all the love duets in Shakespeare's text rolled into one. It is a *vague des passions,* too preconscious, too lacking in explicit declaration of meaning, to be limited to only one scenario. A love duet in words necessarily makes the finite situation clear; but a love duet in music has this advantage, that it can serve indiscriminately for the first brushing-together of virgin hands, and for the last spasm. In the symphonic center of *Roméo et Juliette,* Berlioz took advantage of certain freedoms permitted by his detextualized approach to drama.

The absence of text also leaves the identity of the birds vague, as well—Berlioz didn't have to answer the question, Lark or nightingale? The basic night-music figure at the beginning (measure 125) is a rapid five-note frill, a monotone except that the third note rises a half-step or whole-step above the rest (see example 6). This doesn't sound like a lark: we are audibly in the midst of a nocturne, a veiled musical discourse groping at melody. It is one of several night-aviaries in Berlioz's music: other hypnotic examples include the song *Au cimetière,* from the *Nuits d'été* sequence (1841), with its *roucoulement* of a pale dove; and the duo-nocturne for Héro and Ursule in *Béatrice et Bénédict* (1862), with its bird-sobs, stridulations, chants of

Example 6. Night-birds

the nightingale: *Philomèle Qui mèle Aux murmures du bois Les splendeurs de sa voix* (Philomel who mingles with the murmurs of the wood the splendors of her voice). This last phrase is marked, like much of the duo-nocturne, with a warble of sixteenth notes sung in parallel sixths, rising and falling across a minor second, creating a tremulous effect somewhat similar to that of the five-note frill from *Roméo et Juliette* mentioned above. This suggests that when Berlioz was explicitly evoking a nightingale, he wrote music tinted identically to the night music in the *Roméo et Juliette* adagio. Therefore, in the balcony scene we seem to find ourselves in a nightingale-haunted orchard.

On the other hand, Berlioz was uneasy about nightingales. In 1838—a year before the composition of *Roméo et Juliet*—Berlioz wrote an article on Beethoven's Sixth Symphony, which applauds the bird imitations in the Adagio, except for the nightingale:

> . . . I will say that Beethoven's adversaries seem correct with respect to the nightingale, whose song is no better imitated here than in M. Lebrun's famous flute solo; for the simple reason that the nightingale, making only indeterminate [*inappréciables*] or variable sounds, can't be imitated by instruments with fixed sounds of settled pitch; but it seems to me that this isn't the case for the quail and the cuckoo . . . [their] fixed notes have permitted an exact and complete imitation.[36]

Readers may easily confirm Berlioz's point by listening to the recording of an actual nightingale's song that Respighi wrote into the night scene in *The Pines of Rome*: the bird's song avails itself of notes not in the chromatic scale. Of course the orchestra contains instruments, such as violins and trombones, that *can* vary their sounds continuously between fixed pitches; Berlioz, however, would have hated a more exact imitation of the nightingale's microtones, as his essay on Chinese music suggests:

> What a violin! it's a bamboo tube . . . Between its two strings, lightly twisted around each other, pass the hairs of a fantastic bow . . . These two strings are discordant. . . the Chinese Paganini . . . holding his instrument supported on his knee, uses the fingers of his left hand on the top of the double string in order to vary its intonation, as we do in

playing a cello, but without heeding any division concerning whole-tones, half-tones, or any interval whatsoever. He thus produces a continuous series of gratings, weak meowings, which give the impression of the wailings of the newborn child of a ghoul and a vampire.[37]

Berlioz had little taste for indeterminate pitches. He did like, however, to write music in which "Like objects half-perceived in darkness, its images develop," to cite again the passage from Berlioz's early essay on the *genre instrumental expressif*.[38] So I believe that Berlioz's imagination worked in the following manner: in composing the Adagio of *Roméo et Juliette*, he borrowed the nightingales from the slow movement of Beethoven's Sixth Symphony, not for the sake of quoting their uncertain song, but for the sake of creating an evocation of uncertainty itself. In other words: Berlioz has promoted the concept of nightingale from the level of imitation to the level of structure, in his quest for a nocturnal sort of discourse. He wanted, not vagueness of pitch, but vagueness of text, a musical image of temporal disorientation. In certain Renaissance paintings of Christ's nativity, the painter inserts reminders of the crucifixion—nails, thorns; similarly Berlioz inserts into the very beginning of the adagio proper—the nativity of love— a shadowy pre-audition of the nightingales from the desperate aubade from Shakespeare's third act. Roméo and Juliette are swimming in the whole round of their love-tragedy, darkly co-present in the music.

As our ears accustom themselves to the audible darkness, they begin to discern more human sounds. Always fluctuating, the tempo hesitantly picks up speed, until we reach a section marked *canto appassionato assai* (quite impassioned song); a little later, the passion of the song is momentarily spent, and the music thins to a section marked *col carattere di Recit.* (in the character of recitative)—where Romeo (cello) and Juliet (flute, oboe) lapse into an evocation of speech.[39] Because of the large time-scale of the movement, the music seems to ebb and surge according to biological rhythms, not according to the rigid demarcations of a pre-existing musical template. The pseudo-recitative hints that if passion is too thoroughly exhausted, the adagio will sink back to opera; it can maintain its symphonic nature only through rousing itself with new vertigos of song.

After this, the great melodic excursus begins, a series of swooning arcs, as if Romeo and Juliet were kissing, unkissing, kissing again. It is as if the whole opening part of the adagio—with its tra-las, its bird-calls, its first attempts at serenading, its shy talk—provides a sort of quarry of motives for the construction of an immense song. And here we come to understand how differently Berlioz and Shakespeare conceived young love.

For Shakespeare, love is a conflagration, but a conflagration in which both parties have been carefully trained to burn. Romeo and Juliet have both been reading the same poetry books; they can, at the first moment they meet, complete one another's lines, compose a sonnet together. Shakespeare's lovers can understand one another instantly, devastatingly, for they are textually unison. They know each other's words, before either speaks.

But Berlioz's lovers are more hesitant, and need more time to adjust to one another before they can make their huge musical declaration. They begin with a short-breathed, slightly panting and quizzical musical language, as if they couldn't quite believe in their own happiness; it is not until the middle of the adagio that they can synchronize themselves into a grand melodic span, with phrases longer than any human throat could sing. They don't know their music in advance; it takes a long time before they can put it together, catch each other's tune. Berlioz's lovers are shyer, more awkward, more self-contained in their urgency. Possibly their abandon seems all the more abandoned for being less immediate, more achieved.

Eventually the melody pours itself all out, and we reach a moment of tense expectancy, a prolonged instant of silence—a thirty-second-note rest, with a fermata over it (at measure 307). Then there begins one of Berlioz's most astonishing passages, which starts as a great build-up of an E-major chord. Since the principal key of the adagio is A major, this passage represents a grand move to the dominant; and it feels like a breakthrough onto a higher plane of musical discourse, a sort of transfiguration. Harmonically it is decisive, brilliant; but rhythmically it is oddly indeterminate, since the rising chord is syncopated, and the accompaniment is also syncopated, oddly fluttering; it seems to represent both a hard clasp and some light shudder. The feathery urgency keeps increasing, as the E-major chord tries to attain a sort of transcendence: first by recasting itself in E minor, then by leaping to C major (as the E–G–B chord overreaches itself to E–G–C), then by sinking back to E minor, as if to extract the maximum intensity of pathos; then it recedes and begins a second spurting-upward, this time starting in E minor. One might expect this passage to land on a B chord, the dominant of the dominant, but, instead of finding a chord with a B on the bottom and an F♯ on top, the top note moves up a notch further to produce a chord of B–D–F–G, as if G major could be an altered, red-shifted dominant for E minor. In this fashion the chord keeps overreaching itself, spiralling giddily through several startling mutations, until it dwindles to a few after-throbs on a diminished chord. In the scenario of the balcony scene, this passage represents a confident concord in love. But in other scenarios, this passage means something else—perhaps the first truly effective metaphor for orgasm in the history of music (example 7).[40]

Roméo et Juliette is constructed as a enormous arch; and this erotically charged passage is the high point, the climax. From here on we will be revisiting, in altered form, materials and procedures that we've heard before. Having wound the tension as far as it will go, Berlioz proceeds, from here on, with a long unwinding.

Example 7. Orgasm?

The adagio, as it comes to its conclusion, grows increasingly distracted, fragmentary, as if Romeo and Juliet were becoming unable to sustain their fury of concentration on one another. Near the end of the movement, Rushton hears the voice of the Nurse summoning Juliet back to a more prosaic world[41]—perhaps by analogy with the alba and the aubade, the old dawn songs that warned illicit lovers to end their revels. (A late example can be found in Wagner's Brangaene, whose clarion song fails to persuade Tristan and Isolde that they must part; today it may be difficult to hear Berlioz's love scene without thinking of Wagner.) But in any case, the movement that begins with vague bird-calls ends in wisps and afterthoughts of love.

The hiatal textures of the end of the adagio prepare the listener for Queen Mab, the scherzo of Berlioz's grand symphony. Of course, we've already heard a tenor quote Mercutio's narrative, in the operatic first part of *Roméo et Juliette*; but now Mab has been promoted from a charming character in a silly story to a fiend in Romeo's mind. In the tenor's scherzetto, we were presented with the harmless, fairy-tale version of Mab; now Mab has become a kind of brain disease, a worm that has crawled into Romeo's inner ear, eating away at normal possibilities for coherence in thinking. In the scherzetto, we heard what Mercutio said; in the scherzo, we hear what Romeo heard.

Here Mab escapes from the confines of Mercutio's vaudeville-turn speech, and comes alive. The fantasy of Mab is now wordless, eerie, fully internalized into the instrumental discourse of the symphony—not a mere figment, but as valid and authentic as any other aspect of love's delirium. In the orchestral sections, figures of speech are emancipated from the domain of

Example 8. Mab: diminished seventh in melodic form

tropes, and become wholly realized: Berlioz's music becomes the surrogate for the poetry of Shakespeare, where two stars might wander out of the sky to change positions with Juliet's eyes, where a fairy queen riding in a nutshell has as much dignity as any earthly queen. As much dignity, and much more speed and energy: for she gallops *prestissimo,* at such a lofty height that the bass line often appears in the treble clef; the commonplace prosaic world is almost entirely abandoned, in a fairy music of excluded middles.

This sort of music wasn't quite unprecedented: Mendelssohn's fairy music for *A Midsummer Night's Dream* has a similar deftness, shimmer, and lift. In fact the young Berlioz idly suggested to Mendelssohn in 1831 that it was surprising that no one had written a scherzo on the theme of Queen Mab— and then instantly regretted giving Mendelssohn an idea he wished to reserve for himself.[42] But Berlioz's fairy music is more frenzied, more erratic than Mendelssohn's. Mendelssohn sought speed, delicacy, a sort of eerie propriety fit for a world of overtones; Berlioz sought, above all, a sense of *elusiveness.* The key of Berlioz's scherzo is certainly F major, but the initial skittery melody for violins has strong tendencies to borrow notes from other keys; and its very first statement concludes in mid-air (C#), via a melodic figure that seems be spun out of a diminished seventh chord (example 8). This aerial chatter is regularly interrupted by chords, sometimes consisting of normal triads, but often consisting of a diminished seventh chord, moving bizarrely from one configuration of itself to another (before at last finding a resolution): a harmonically static experiment with shifts of timbre and color, as if Queen Mab were briefly poised, iridescing. On other occasions a note will suddenly sustain itself, while high notes dance from an octave to a major ninth to a minor ninth above. The unpredictability of this music continues to amaze, even after long acquaintance.

The scherzo is one long dissolve. In the adagio, Romeo and Juliet found their tune; but in the scherzo, we enter an almost tuneless and figureless musical domain. It is as if Romeo remains aroused, but can't hang onto any clear shape of love; he dwells in Coleridge's limbo, a state of intense imaginativeness that hovers between images without coming to rest. The music of Queen Mab becomes an alternate construction of the whole love scene, exhilarating but also disturbing.

At the trio, marked Allegretto, the tiny rapid gallop slows down by a factor of three,[43] and the key moves from F to the relative minor, D; trills seem to represent cricket chirps and other insect noises, as Berlioz's focus seems to shift to the grasshopper covers and cricket's-bone whips that adorn the fairy carriage—but the galloping can't be stopped long, and the prestissimo resumes. Soon we start to hear fairy horn calls; and then comes a remarkable passage that might be called a second trio, although there is no change of tempo or other sectional indication in the score. Here Berlioz extracts falling fifths from the F minor and D♭ major triads, and keeps equivocating between major and minor. This bit of shadowy ambiguity was lifted from an early choral song, *Ballet des ombres* (1829):

Formez vos rangs, entrez en danse!	Form your rows and start to dance!
L'ombre descend, le jour s'enfuit.	Shadow descends, and day takes flight.
Hou!	Hoo!
Ombres, votre règne commence	Ghosts, now your reign begins
Dans la sombre horreur da la nuit.	In the black horror of the night.
Hou!	Hoo!

When Berlioz re-orchestrated this passage for the scherzo, he called for antique cymbals, another way of exploring the far ranges of otherness in Western music. The adagio pertains to Juliet's presence; the scherzo pertains to Juliet's absence, a sort of distention of imagination, like gas released into a vacuum. This ghost-ballet, in which a funeral knell is accelerated into Halloween revels, is perfectly appropriate for Mab's retinue; but the anxious possibility remains that Juliet herself has become a ghost, in anticipation of her actual burial. Unsubstantial death, that lean abhorrèd monster, has already turned Juliet into his paramour. Because circumstances prevented any just expectation of a long secure marriage, the lovers were always somewhat unreal to each other; and in the scherzo Juliet has already started to dance out of Romeo's grasp, to refigure herself as something amorphous, delirious. Ever since the operatic section 1 ended, Romeo has dwelt in a wordless, dangerously ungrounded domain, a continual shape-shifting of chimeras of love, chimeras of fear; and, as the symphonic sections 2, 3, and 4 end, this phantasmagorical state is becoming explicit. It is difficult for instrumental music to retain semantic clarity; and this precariousness of meaning finally overwhelms the whole implied sensibility of Romeo, our protagonist (example 9).

Queen Mab, in the scherzetto at the end of section 1, inaugurated the mysteries of love; now Mab, at the end of section 4, dispels those same mysteries, and leaves Romeo high sorrowful and cloyed. What begins as inspiration must end as a hollow image. The symphony seems to confess

Example 9. Mab's umbral regions

that it needs something more, in order to make itself explicit. As we've seen, the purpose of the Mab speech, in Shakespeare, is to bring Romeo back to earth, to call attention to the silliness of the cherished figments of love, to wake him up. In *L'île inconnue,* the final song in *Les nuits d'été* (1841—not long after *Roméo et Juliette*), Berlioz set a charming Gautier poem in which a lover invites his *jeune belle* to sail with him to Java or Norway or anywhere at all, in a boat with an oar made of ivory, a rudder of gold, a sail spun from an angel's wing—and, for ballast, a single orange. The whole vehicular form of this contraption seems a nautical re-imagining of the chariot of Queen Mab. At the end of the poem, the girl asks him to take her to the shores where love lasts forever; but the poet delicately declines, for no one seems to know the directions to that place. Extravagant tropes are put to flight by a canny, self-conscious mind; the poet's dreams fume away, and the critic wakes up. By the end of the Queen Mab scherzo in *Roméo et Juliette,* the composer seems to have reached a similar impasse; and so we fall out of the reverie of symphony, and into the vigilance of opera.

4. *Roméo et Juliette*: The Opera Resumes

At the end of Berlioz's section 1, we had not yet come to the end of Shakespeare's first act; Berlioz's exposition of the plot corresponds to Shakespeare's prologue sonnet, and is wholly anticipatory in character. As section 5 begins, we are already in the domain of the last act. The whole inner drama of *Romeo and Juliet* occurs in the symphonic sections 2, 3, and 4—another reason for believing that the adagio corresponds not just to the balcony scene, but to every intimate scene between the lovers.

We are in the domain of the last act—but Garrick's last act, not Shakespeare's, as Berlioz explicitly noted:

Without doubt Garrick found the right dénouement for *Romeo and Juliet,* containing the greatest degree of pathos that the theatre can provide;

this ending has replaced Shakespeare's, which has a less gripping effect; but by contrast, what sort of insolent clown devised the [happy] dénouement for *King Lear,* sometimes, even often, substituted for the scene that Shakespeare outlined for this masterwork?[44]

Berlioz preferred Garrick's treatment of the last act of *Romeo and Juliet,* but thought that almost all other tamperings with the masters were wretched and reprehensible. It is possible to see why Berlioz would call attention to Garrick: Garrick demonstrated (according to Berlioz) that it was possible to improve Shakespeare, and therefore gave a kind of warrant for Berlioz's own subliminal project of competing with Shakespeare.

The opera of sections 5, 6, and 7 opens with a funeral procession—*Convoi funèbre de Juliette*—with the odd (though perfectly exact) sub-heading, "Fugal March, first for instruments, with a psalmody on just one note in the voices; then for voices, with the psalmody in the orchestra." This procession, complete with comparisons of Juliet to a flower cut before its time, was entirely the idea of Garrick, who wished to make Juliet's death a more public and spectacular occasion for sentiment: in 1750 Garrick commissioned William Boyce to write (quite beautiful) music for his fu-neral procession scene, complete with the steady tolling of a bell. Of course, it must be remembered that this cortège pertains only to the death simu-lated by the poison; Juliet is still alive, and will soon awake. In some sense, we're still in the realm of Queen Mab, the ruler of fictitious and unreal affection, and Berlioz's extraordinary ingenuity of form does impart a cer-tain sense of contrivance; but the choral mourning seems sincere enough, as it should, since the Capulet mourners believe Juliet to be truly dead. Berlioz evidently considered the break between section 4 (Mab) and sec-tion 5 to be the strongest point of division in the score: at the first perfor-mance there was an intermission before the funeral procession (itself pre-ceded by the deleted second choral prologue). And the lethargy and the solemnity of the funeral procession seem remote indeed from Mab's scherzo; the force of gravity is increasing as we approach the world of opera, which is (for Berlioz's purposes in this work) ceremonious, heavy-footed, the op-posite of fantasy. We are on the verge of rejoining a more serious, more tedious, more legalistic universe. This effect was especially strong at the first performance, in which this movement ended with a chanted *Requiem aeternam* (later deleted), as if the church were gathering its strength to coopt love-fantasy, break it on the grid of pre-established ritual.

In the field of instrumental music familiar in the early nineteenth cen-tury, a slow movement might seem amorous (as in Beethoven's Fourth Sym-phony, as Berlioz heard it) or funereal (as in Beethoven's Third); and it would be possible to construe the *Convoi funèbre* as a sort of alternate slow movement to the symphonic parts of *Roméo et Juliette.* The funeral procession equivocates nicely between the symphonic and the operatic. Even the texture of the piece, in which the chorus and the orchestral neatly trade places in the middle (first the chorus gives a pedal-point to the orchestra, then the orchestra gives a pedal-point to the chorus), proves that voices can easily do the work of instruments, and instruments can easily do the work of voices. The listener is in a border region between the vocal and the orchestral, between opera and symphony, an indistinct land between genres; but the order of the two halves suggests that instruments are waning in importance, and voices waxing, as symphony gives way to opera. In the adagio, we heard the sleepy voices of the revelers leaving the ball, vanishing in the distance, as a preparation for a world of voiceless intensities; now, the chorus starts to waken, in a gentle lament, as a preparation for a world of loud and insistent voices, in the operatic finale.

But what firmly places the *Convoi funèbre* in Part Three is its key. Section 1, if it has a distinct key at all, is in B minor; the symphony of sections 2, 3, and 4, is clearly in F major; and, as we'll see, section 7 finishes strongly in B major. The first half of the *Convoi funèbre* is in E minor, and the second half in E major, the subdominant of B major; this choice of key firmly distances the *Convoi funèbre* from symphony and affiliates it with opera—a lower, less intense domain, in Berlioz's scheme for this work. Harmonically, Berlioz has already begun the process of saying goodbye to Romeo and Juliet; the music is dissociating itself from love, and affiliating itself with the society of Verona and its pre-established rites for mourning.

Section 6 is entitled *Roméo au tombeau des Capulets,* and is, by general consent, the most original part of the entire score. Berlioz himself seems to have considered it too challenging for many audiences, for he noted that it "should be cut in 99 out of 100 performances."[45]

Its challenge lies chiefly in its disruptiveness of musical form: it is a bundle of clonic musical gestures, following Garrick's scenario for the tomb scene: *Invocation—Awakening of Juliet—Delirious joy, despair—Last agonies and death of the two lovers.* (In Shakespeare's text, Romeo and Juliet have no opportunity to talk with each other in the tomb.) It is the only moment in the score where Romeo and Juliet are "present," not in a symphony, but in an opera—but an opera without singers, for Berlioz strictly observes his premise that the lovers dwell on a plane beyond the singable. Its musical antecedents therefore can be found in incidental music to plays—except that musical instruments are not accompanying speech, not underscoring dumb show, but impersonating voices and embodying physiology. The movement is one of the most remarkable acts of transvestism between orchestra and human body ever devised. For this brief span the social opera of Verona is interrupted by a new kind of operatic experience, a *somatic opera.*

I propose the term *somatic opera* along lines suggested by Roland Barthes, in his beautiful essay "Rasch": Barthes speaks of the *somathemes* in

Schumann, by which he means the music of pulse-throbs and biceps-contractions:

> In Schumann's *Kreisleriana* (Opus 16; 1838), I actually hear no note, no theme, no contour, no grammar, no meaning, nothing which would permit me to reconstruct an intelligible structure of the work. No, what I hear are blows: I hear what beats in the body, what beats the body, or better: I hear this body that beats.[46]

Kreisleriana, of course, has notes, themes, and grammar—it is simply that the body implied by the music resounds more loudly in Barthes' ears than the the notes, the themes, the grammar. But in *Roméo au tombeau* there really *is* little in the way of theme, and almost nothing in the way of grammar—the music seems to be a string of disconnected harsh or pathetic gestures; and in the absence of theme and grammar, the bodies of Romeo and Juliet surge to the foreground. The movement is a kind of musical stethoscope.

There was a strong aspect of corporeality in the sexually charged slow movement, but a corporeality different from that of *Roméo au tombeau.* In the adagio, the pulse's acceleration, the heart's tumescences, were bodied forth through an orchestral song; but in *Roméo au tombeau,* the physiology is not a complement to a musical structure, but a force opposing any musical structure. Love seems to invite music, but death seems to resist music, in any connected and melodious sense of the word. We have reached a place where musical expression and musical form are antithetical. On the frontiers of music, the orchestra becomes a sort of recording device for spastic contractions, for paroxysms of the brain. By the end of this movement, Berlioz is devising audible images for the death-rattle, for the loosening of muscle tonus, for sickening things in the belly. Schoenberg's *Erwartung* (1909), a madwoman's monodrama, in which "atonal" music follows the exact contours of psychic pain, can be glimpsed on the horizon of *Roméo au tombeau.*

But this sort of physiologically engorged music looks to the past as well as the future. Berlioz was not the first composer to write music constructed around heartbeat figures—perhaps in the overture and finale of Mozart's *Don Giovanni* (1787) we can even hear the beat of a statue's implacable heart. A more explicit heart-notation can be found in the operatic invention, at the end of the eighteenth century, of a sort of heartbeat-recitative— a heartbeat disengaged from other musical phenomena, a rhythmic figure promoted into a monotone in the foreground. For example, in the quartet of Méhul's *Stratonice* (1792)—a number that Berlioz admired greatly[47]— there is a section where a doctor performs a physical exam: as he takes the pulse, iambic figures in the strings rise up against the (oddly cheerful) wood-

Example 10. Berlioz's notation of his own heartbeat.

wind music of the general orchestral texture. It isn't far from this rather gentle musical medicine to the physiological exactitude of Berlioz's *La mort de Cléopâtre* (1829), where, as the poison takes effect, we hear the queen's horribly loud pulse, first labored, then thready. Berlioz performed a full emancipation of the heartbeat: but perhaps every opera is, to some degree, a somatic opera. By 1847 Berlioz was so heartbeat-obsessed that he sent a letter to Liszt describing how, during a successful Russian performance of *Roméo et Juliette,* "I felt my heart clench itself [*se serrer*] in the middle of the adagio," and further went to the trouble of notating the rhythm of the "nervous trembling" of his heart, a series of irregular triplets (example 10).[48]

Of course, *Roméo au tombeau* engages, not only an implied body, but an implied mind: we hear Romeo experiencing his delirious joy and despair in terms of music heard previously in the dramatic symphony. And yet, a word such as *reminiscence* doesn't seem right to describe the process of musical recall: a reminiscence is a savoring of temporality, a mellow awareness of the discrepancy between past and presence, whereas *Roméo au tombeau* is immediate, sheer, bristling. I will mention two instances of Berlioz's sinister thematic recalls. First, in the section marked *Reveil de Juliette,* an out-of-breath clarinet seems to be trying to play (and almost succeeding in playing) Juliet's distinctively hesitant love-melody (clarinet and English horn) from measure 127 of the love scene. (This theme is also heard, in a varied form, in the shy flutes and oboes of the *allegro agitato* of the love scene; it is related to the call of the night-bird discussed earlier). In the adagio, Juliet seemed to be communing with the night; now she seems to communing with the deepest night of all. As Chailley has noticed,[49] this chromatic theme was originally heard in the Prologue, when the chorus sang *Le jeune Roméo, plaignant sa destinée*—the tune is first anticipated, then experienced, at last, effortfully, resuscitated. Second (this is the instance illustrated below in examples 11 and 12), in the section marked *Joie délirante,* the orchestra plays (at measure 35) an immensely speeded-up version of the *canto appassionato assai* from the adagio. In the first instance, the theme is eaten away by long pauses and by sinister runs in the strings, as Thanatos overcomes Eros; in the second example, as we can see, the theme attempts to escape from time by compressing itself into a single moment of peak intensity: if the *canto appassionato assai* theme were played any more rapidly, it would be the flicker of a chord, not a melody at all.

[Allegro vivace ed appassionato assai]

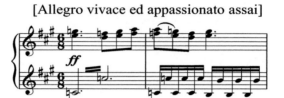

Example 11. Delirious joy in the tomb

Example 12. *Canto appassionato assai* from the love scene: source of example 11

In the large arch of *Roméo et Juliette, Roméo au tombeau* is thematically parallel to the adagio, in that it revisits and erases the great love themes; but it is structurally parallel to the catalogue section of the Prologue. There, we heard an anticipation of the symphonic themes, cuing us in mapping the symphony onto Shakespeare's play; here, we hear the themes dismantling themselves, receding into themelessness. In the *Symphonie fantastique,* the concluding rondo of witches' sabbath desecrated the beloved, reduced her, by means of thematic parody, to a whore. Romeo and Juliet aren't caricatured; but the parody of their love themes breaks down the lovers, leaves them unable to sustain themselves in the midst of death's stern musicological analysis. In his Prix de Rome cantata *La mort d'Orphée* (1827), Berlioz wrote a graphic musical depiction of the dismemberment of Orpheus; and in *Roméo au tombeau,* Romeo is similarly torn limb from limb, in a sort of *sparagma* of the music of the adagio. The symphony of sections 2, 3, and 4 is broken up and dismissed, in preparation for the operatic finale, where Romeo and Juliet are dead, and none of their music is henceforth available to be heard.

So we see that *Roméo au tombeau* says both farewell to the symphony, and hello to the operatic finale. As an introduction to the finale, *Roméo au tombeau* clearly alludes to the introduction to the finale of Beethoven's Ninth Symphony, its most striking formal precedent, in that Beethoven begins his finale with harsh and peremptory gestures; then recalls themes from the preceding movements; then resumes the disruptive clamor; and at last settles into the *concordia discors* of the Ode to Joy, as chaos resolves into cosmos. In 1838—not long before writing *Roméo et Juliette*—Berlioz confessed that he was utterly unable to understand why Beethoven began his finale with sheer noise: "ALL THE NOTES OF THE MINOR DIA-TONIC SCALE are struck at the same time, producing a fearsome assemblage of sounds: F, A, C♯, E, G, B♭, D."[50] Berlioz notes that, in Jean Paul Égide Martini's opera *Sapho*, a similar auditory overload occurs to accompany the heroine's suicidal plunge into the sea, in which case the expressive intent is unmistakable; but Beethoven's discord leaves him puzzled.

I believe that *Roméo au tombeau* is Berlioz's attempt to understand the beginning of Beethoven's finale by repeating its gestures in a clearly specified interpretive frame. Berlioz (like some other critics of his generation) tried to understand Beethoven's symphonies as occluded expressions of Shakespeare or Dante; here, Berlioz in effect created a story for Beethoven's incomprehensible music, then rewrote the music in order to make it better fit the story. He retained the structural essence of Beethoven's opening for his finale, the combination of loud disruption and thematic recall; but Berlioz's music is so semantically explicit that no one asks, What does this mean?—to hear it, especially with Berlioz's minutely annotated score in hand, is to *know* what it means.

The finale proper is both the most and the least Shakespearean part of Berlioz's score—the most Shakespearean, in that Berlioz at last provides a vocal enactment of a full scene, with a bass who doesn't *quote* Friar Lawrence (in the sense that the tenor previously quoted Mercutio), but actually *plays* Friar Lawrence, confronting the Capulets and Montagues; the least Shakespearean, in that Berlioz's obedience to operatic conventions makes us more conscious of recent musical precedents (the oath scene in Rossini's *Guillaume Tell* [1829], and so forth) than of Shakespeare's old play. Furthermore, Berlioz's Lawrence, terrifying and authoritative, is scarcely to be recognized as Shakespeare's distracted puttering klutz.

In the symmetrical form of the whole *Roméo and Juliet,* the end is like the beginning—and the finale indeed starts as a second version of the Introduction. The Capulets and Montagues are still brawling, as if nothing had happened at all. At first there is aimless confusion, as the bewildered chorus cries out for Lawrence to elucidate the deaths of the lovers; Lawrence calmly explains; then the chorus becomes decisive, and calls for blood, as orchestra resumes the feud-fugue, first heard in the opening bars of the work. There, Prince Escalus, impersonated by the low brass, shouted down the mob; here, it is the church, in the form of Lawrence, that hurls down the thunderbolt of Jove: *Silence, malheureux!* Perhaps Berlioz, native to a Roman Catholic country, could find somewhat more gubernatorial force in the church than Shakespeare could easily imagine from the shattered monasteries of the Church of Rome, or the very young institutions of the Church of England.

Roméo et Juliette concludes with an assertion of law—the law of the church, made audible in a great hymn-tune:

Jurez donc, par l'auguste symbole,	Swear then, by the high symbol of God,
Sur le corps de la fille et sur le corps du fils,	On the girl's body and the body of the son,
Par ce bois douloureux qui console,	By this consoling sign, this holy rood,
Jurez tous, jurez par le saint crucifix.	All swear, swear by this cross of pain.

This grand anthem (example 13) is conclusive in two senses. First, it establishes an irrefutable key of B major, demonstrating that *Roméo et Juliette* consists of a symphony in F major embedded within an opera in B minor / major—just the sort of large-scale tritonal relationship not usually permitted in tonal music. The symphony is skewed on a harmonic plane orthogonal to that of the opera—a device for proving in harmony the theorem that Romeo and Juliet *don't belong* to the same system as the rest of Verona. It is a procedure for demonstrating the starkly enforced separation between the love code, with its symphonic commingling of themes, and the social code, with its operatic divisions into self-contained musical segments. (There is an odd sequel to this B vs. F harmonic schema in Gounod's *Roméo et Juliette* [1867]: the nocturne that begins the second act is in F, while Romeo's *Ah lève-toi, soleil* is in the startling key of B major—Gounod used the tritonally related keys to symbolize the opposition between night and day.)

Second, *Jurez donc* is a conspicuously steady, impregnable sort of melody, a melody on which Lawrence and the chorus can rely, conclude. Pursuing the analogy with Beethoven's Ninth, we might say that *Jurez donc* plays the role of the Ode to Joy tune, summarizing and embracing. But this analogy is fragile. *Freude, schöner Götterfunken* is in some respects a less interesting tune than *Jurez donc*, but it is infinitely more flexible, more suscep-

Andante un poco maestoso (♩. = 54)

Ju - rez donc___ par l'au - gus - te sym - bo - le,

Sur___ le corps___ de la fille et sur le corps du fils,

Example 13. Swear!

tible to variation; it can be made an image of the spinning universe precisely because it can be transmogrified into a sweet hymn, a Turkish march,
an abyss of silence—anything at all. But there's little that Berlioz (or perhaps anyone else) could do with *Jurez donc* except to make it louder. It
belongs to the class of pompous, orotund Berlioz melodies, of the sort familiar from the *Symphonie funèbre et triomphale* and other musical ceremonies designed for political or ecclesiastical occasions. It is memorable,
even fascinating, because of its swerves from B major to C$\sharp$ minor (at *le
corps du fils*) and G$\sharp$ minor (at *saint crucifix*); but the unusualness of the
harmonic pattern only increases its rigidity, for the melody has all its com-
plexity built in; further complexifying would be an unwelcome interfer-
ence with its oath-compelling solemnity.

In this fashion Berlioz ends *Roméo et Juliette* with a general adoration
of the Law. It is a little as if Wagner had ended *Die Meistersinger* by killing
off the noble young Walther, and awarding Eva's hand to an overjoyed
Beckmesser (the carping legalist)—for nothing in Shakespeare's play makes
us confident that the Law, either of the church or of the State, is an effica-
cious instrument in dealing with human passion. But perhaps, for Berlioz,
passion could triumph only in the world of symphony; and opera was such
a recalcitrant, stiff, vexatious genre that it declares that Friar Lawrence
and Prince Escalus are the true heroes of a Romeo and Juliet opera.

2. Eugène Delacroix. *Mephistopheles Hovering over the City.*

IV

Goethe's *Faust*

1. Introduction

In 1828 there appeared two French translations of Goethe's *Faust*. The one that everyone remembers is by Gérard de Nerval, a mad poet attracted to such magical eccentrics as Faust. The other one, the second edition of a dry translation by one Albert Stapfer, would be forgotten except for its illustrations by Eugène Delacroix, including the famous lithograph *Mephistopheles Hovering over the City*.

In some respects Delacroix's image is all wrong for Goethe. Mephistopheles is depicted as a writhing Titan, naked except for his jaunty peaked hat. Eyelidless, nearly lipless, smiling, he seems extremely exposed, as if all the world's evil were manifest above us, an evil so large that the city below looks made of toy buildings. The figure is too powerful and Satanic for Goethe, who told an actor taking the part of Mephistopheles to play him in an elegant, baronial style, not with demonic grimaces.[1] Goethe's Mephistopheles is a subtle disputant, relaxed, ironical—and irony, as in the Greek New Comedy, is ultimately a rhetoric for slaves, not for masters. Goethe makes Mephistopheles aware of his servile condition; but Delacroix's Mephistopheles is a tortured god.

But other aspects of Delacroix's image respond to Goethe's poem with precision. Formally, the picture is a dialectic of points: the church spires want to skewer the hovering body, but are too flimsy and insubstantial; their uprightness is everywhere contradicted, annulled, by the sharp diagonals of fingernails, toenails, knees, ankles, chin, pointing every which way but straight. Mephistopheles' wings seem too steeply bent to assist with the act of flight: instead they provide further means for pointing, for gesturing at new misleading directions. Goethe's Mephistopheles is just like that: he understands Faust as a long-legged cicada, "that always flies and, while flying, hops" (l. 289); and the proper job of a tempter is to point wrong, to confuse direction. Everywhere Delacroix creates zigzags, by splaying limbs, by bending joints at sharp angles: Mephistopheles' right wrist is so tensely turned up that he seems about to play a chord, as if the whole city were a keyboard under his hand. The outline of his body is everywhere jagged: he personifies a path that leads nowhere.

Furthermore, he manages to disturb and to darken the air around him. Delacroix drew shadings around Mephistopheles that echo his shape, especially around his left wing, as if he were exerting a plastic stress on the atmosphere itself, convulsing it with visible tremors. Indeed the whole huge body seems to be a thickening of the ether, an inflection of sky, the human form of a lightning bolt waiting to fall. Mephistopheles seems to constitute his own universe, or quaquaverse. And this loss of a clear boundary between an object and the medium in which the object appears is, as we'll see, a pictorial strategy appropriate for Goethe's *Faust*. *Faust* is a very German poem; and German art is the art of fields, not the art of distinct forms.

2. Getting Lost in Domains of Desire

Heinrich Wölfflin, in *Italien und das deutsche Formgefühl* (1931) understood Italian art as the clear, crisp deployment of isolated (or isolatable) geometrical forms, and understood German art as essentially the bulging and buckling of great planes and volumes. Wölfflin spoke of German figural groups in which human bodies are "powerful breakers of a swirling surf of foam"; of German drawings in which a "saint is like a spider in a web of lines and lights"; of German architecture in which "something spins down from the ceiling and stirs in the nooks and corners"[2]—it is an art in which space is continually invading and assaulting the figures that occupy it, in which figure and ground constitute a whorling unitary system, like the vortices of Descartes or Leibniz, ever whirligigging the planets around the sun.

Goethe conceived Faust in the same way that the Old Masters of German drawing conceived their images. Wölfflin described how Schongauer's Saint Sebastian is difficult to distinguish from the tree behind him: Sebastian seems to *fray*, as if his bark were starting to peel off.[3] The human body leaks out, engorges itself, into the surrounding tissue of things: the drawing posits a single system of flesh and landscape. Similarly Goethe's Faust inhabits a world that so accommodates itself to his wishes that it is simply a magnified image of his whole system of appetite and revulsion. Mephistopheles operates as a sort of amplifier, increasing the potency of the electromagnetic field of desire that Faust generates around himself. Most of us live in such circumscribed, cramped worlds that we are more aware of the frustration of desire than of desire itself; but in the laboratory of *Faust*, Goethe allows his protagonist to come to a full awareness of himself through a full exercise of will—a will that can twist, deform, the contours of the universe around it. How does a man know who he is?—not through what he does, not through what he thinks, but through what he *wants*; therefore the genie that gratifies wishes brings to light the deepest component of human identity. In this sense Goethe's poem is altogether Romantic.

Every retelling of the Faust story is a study in the quality of desire. Goethe came to know the Faust story during his childhood in Frankfurt, by means of puppet shows distantly derived from Marlowe's *Dr. Faustus* (c. 1593). Later in life Goethe made a close study of many of the earlier versions of the tale. But Goethe's Faust, even as portrayed in the fairly traditional Part One (1808 and 1826—a fragmentary version appeared in 1790), bears surprisingly little resemblance to Marlowe's, or to Marlowe's ultimate source (the collection of tales about Faustus published by Johann Spiess in the famous chapbook of 1587), in that Goethe's Faust has a more refined, more sinuous and self-contradictory system of desire.

All Fausts are children, caught up in childish fantasies of omnipotence; but the sixteenth-century Fausts are exceptionally gross in their childishness. In one of the old stories, Faustus swallows a load of hay, and then a horse and a wagon; in another, he opens his mouth wide and gulps an impertinent young man whole—and then excretes him, alive, unharmed, and wet. Just as the vivacity of babies seems concentrated entirely in their lips, in the great buccinator muscles in their cheeks, so the original Faustus seems to be gigantic mouth, with unhingeable jaws like a python's. He roams the world looking for things to swallow; indeed he roams beyond the world's limits, pulled up on a chariot of dragons above the circle of the moon, until the earth appears "No bigger than my hand in quantity" (Marlowe, 3.1.73)[4]—perhaps Faustus's ultimate ambition is simply to pop the world-ball into his mouth. As Joseph Conrad, in *Heart of Darkness* (1898), wrote of Kurtz—a very Faustian character—"I saw him open his mouth wide—it gave him a weirdly voracious aspect, as though he had wanted to swallow all the air, all the earth. . . ."[5] We see, then, that even at its origin, the Faustus legend is German in Wölfflin's special sense of the word: there are no clear boundaries between Faustus and the world he inhabits, the world he tries to incorporate into himself.

As a baby well past puberty, Faustus is a strolling penis as well as a mouth. In Marlowe's version, Faustus's very first wish, after the agreement to the contract, is as follows: "let me have a wife, the fairest maid in Germany, for I am wanton and lascivious" (2.1.141–42); Mephistopheles, not liking any talk of such sacramental matters as marriage, replies "I'll fetch thee a wife in the devil's name. *Enter with a devil dressed like a woman, with fireworks*" (2.1.146). Faustus is repelled, but mollified at the promise of an endless succession of courtesans. Mephistopheles delivers the courtesans he promises: we even see, during the pageant of the Seven Deadly Sins, Lechery herself, "one that loves an inch of raw mutton, better than an ell of fried stockfish" (2.2.160–61). Lechery may also be a devil dressed like a woman; and the possibility is open that all the objects of Faustus's sexual desire are simply transvestite devils—it is almost as if Mephistopheles himself were a sort of wife, and his contract with Faust a ghastly parody of a marriage ceremony. The devil offers an endless succession of surrogates for objects of desire; Faust is increasingly surrounded by mirages, by spirits that enact dumb-shows, such as the pantomime of Alexander the Great and his courtesan performed for the delight of the emperor (4.2). Sometimes Faustus is conscious of the purely illusory character of what he beholds—"These are but shadows, not substantial" (4.2.55); but on other occasions he forgets himself, and takes the shadow for a solid thing, as when he sees Helen of Troy—"Was this the face that launched a thousand ships? . . . Her lips suck forth my soul, see where it flies!" (5.1.96, 99).

This moment—one of the great leaps of imagination in the whole Elizabethan theatre—is also the one passage in the play when Marlowe's Faustus sounds like Goethe's Faust, that is, rather confused. The novelty of Goethe's sorcerer lies in that he is continually perplexed by the difficulty in distinguishing the hallucinatory from the real; whereas Marlowe's Faustus baffles others, Goethe's Faust baffles himself. The older Faustuses are self-conscious magicians, prestidigitators, rejoicing in the power of deceit and buffoonery. Marlowe's Faustus talks big: caught up in fantasies of re-engineering the whole landscape of Europe, he boasts that "I'll have them wall all Germany with brass, / And make swift Rhine, circle fair Wittenberg" (1.1.87–88). But during the play he contents himself with clown tricks, such as boxing the Pope's ears (3.2.87) or attaching cuckold's-horns to the head of a drunken knight (4.2.73). Faustus is particularly expert with prop prostheses: in one scene he contrives to wear a fake head, so that an enemy can chop it off with a sword (4.3.43)—soon Faustus jumps up in a parody of resurrection, avenges himself on his supposed murderer; in another scene he contrives to wear a fake leg, so that a swindled horse trader, trying to wake Faustus by tugging at his leg, will be comically horrified when the leg comes off (4.6.34). Stray body parts of Faustus are multiplying dangerously—another sort of Wölfflin-like smearing of the distinction between figure and ground—but it is all calculated burlesque, stunts performed with obvious pasteboard head and leg. Marlowe's Faustus dreams of becoming master of the universe, but winds up as the master of ceremonies of magic-show so gimmicky and exposed that no apprentice Houdini would try it—he'd be laughed off the stage. It is farce, but farce so labored that it has an almost Brechtian quality; and indeed Brecht perhaps remembered Marlowe's stage business in his 1929 play, *Das Badener Lehrstück vom Einverständnis*, in which the gull Herr Schmitt enters with a huge head and clumsy stilt-like legs, so that the sharpers can have the pleasure of hacking his limbs off, one by one.

But Goethe's *Faust* is not a farce—it is a much odder thing, a hilarious tragedy. And Goethe's protagonist is not a clown, except insofar as he is himself the object of his own befooling—Faust is the sort of character that the German poet Novalis called a wizard lost in his own labyrinth.

Marlowe's Faustus craves power, authority, and general enslavement of the human race—many of Marlowe's protagonists are like that, especially

Tamburlaine, who uses the defeated emperor Bajazeth as his footstool, and likes to compare himself favorably with Jupiter. But Goethe's Faust is a far more affable character, in that he craves self-improvement: he sells his soul, so to speak, for the sake of personal instruction by the world's most distinguished professor, the professor who's won all the teaching awards, on the whole curriculum of culture. Of course, this curriculum doesn't involve book learning—*that* Faust already knows, and has discarded—but instead involves a sentimental education, and first-hand contact with the source materials of civilization in the West. Prof. Mephistopheles teaches you about love by providing you with a genuine young woman, with guaranteed depth of commitment to your happiness; and he teaches you about culture, not by taking you to the British Museum and pointing to the battered remains of the frieze of the Parthenon, as cheaper professors do, but by actually whizzing you to classical Greece, and introducing you to centaurs and sibyls. Marlowe was a spy and a political intriguer, whose death in tavern brawl, at the age of twenty-nine, may have been an assassination; and so he conceived Faust as the ultimate spy, cloaked with invisibility, capable of twiddling Pope and emperor, of exposing the essential idiocy of politics. But Goethe's *Faust* is an academical sort of book, indeed more academical than Goethe's own biography might warrant: the text seems like the reverie of a harassed college instructor who has to teach five courses each term, and wishes to sweep the books off his desk—Away with you, philosophy, jurisprudence, medicine!—and to fly off campus with an all-knowing guide to tell him the meaning of life, the ideal subject for his dissertation, and the most effective lines for picking up girls.

When I myself was a beginner in the academic racket, a wise elder told me that literature was all about Reality and Illusion, and used quotations from *The Tempest* and Keats's "The Eve of St. Agnes" to support his point. But this is the one kind of instruction that Prof. Mephistopheles can't provide: as Faust's domain of experience distends, as his desires reach toward various sorts of experimental fulfillments, he increasingly loses any sense of terra firma. Marlowe's Faustus manipulated shadows for an earthy sort of purpose—he wanted to be an autocrat; Goethe's Faust wants to be a poet, and to live inside a poem. He abjures his academic and medical career in favor of becoming a figment of his own imagination; and as he turns literary, he turns self-consciously unreal. To some extent he adores the exciting, irresponsible phantasmagoria to which he surrenders himself. A college teacher is always hemmed in, blinkered by the truth, by the need to be faithful to the material that he's teaching; but a poet can exuberate into a completely unstructured realms of contentless creativity.

Goethe's Faust is one of the first of a whole series of Romantic characters who get swallowed up in their own imaginative worlds—a condition best described by W. H. Auden, in *The Sea and the Mirror* (1944):

All the phenomena of an empirically ordinary world are given. Extended objects appear to which events happen—old men catch dreadful coughs, little girls get their arms twisted, flames run whooping through woods, round a river bend, as harmless looking as a dirty old bearskin rug, comes the gliding fury of a town-effacing wave, but these are merely elements in an allegorical landscape to which mathematical measurement and phenomenological analysis have no relevance.

All the voluntary movements are possible—crawling through flues and old sewers, sauntering past shop fronts, tiptoeing through quicksands and mined areas, running through derelict factories and across empty plains, jumping over brooks, diving into pools . . . but any sense of direction, any knowledge of where on earth one has come from or where on earth one is going to is completely absent. . . . Everything, in short, suggests Mind but, surrounded by an infinite extension of the adolescent difficulty, a rising of the subjective and subjunctive to ever steeper, stormier heights, the panting frozen expressive gift has collapsed under the strain of its communicative anxiety, and contributes nothing by way of meaning but a series of staccato barks or a delirious gush of glossolalia.[6]

Here Auden speaks of the pathology of too much imagination—the disease that happens when Ariel gains complete control of the poet, and inspires a sort of willed autism, a condition in which the solid earth dissolves into soft lumps of play-dough, plastic caressive surfaces that offer no resistance to fantasy. What Auden calls Ariel, Goethe calls Mephistopheles: the spirit that liquefies and liquidates, converts the big inert world into a locus of gratification, an evolving hologram that shapes itself according to whim. This role in no way contradicts Mephistopheles' famous self-description,

> I am the spirit that always denies!
> and properly so; all things that come to be
> deserve to perish utterly;
> better nothing were made at all. (ll. 1338–41)[7]

The Romantics conceived the imagination (in Coleridge's words) as a faculty that "dissolves, diffuses, dissipates, in order to re-create":[8] a doctrine that suggests that the necessary preliminary to re-creation is de-creation or un-creation. As a spirit of imagination, Mephistopheles smears out the normal contours of things, so that Faust's will has room to operate. In normal life, the world's old song is "Do without! Thou shalt do without!" (l. 1549); but Mephistopheles offers a domain in which every itch is quickly scratched. Nevertheless, this new domain of gratified desires is not a true re-creation, but something jejune, at once sticky and slippery, dreamlike in the desultory and disoriented way that Auden evokes in his passage on the Ariel-haunted poet. The universe of fantasy is in a sense pre-denied, a brief thickening of the general nothing. The hologram is a hollowgram.

3. The Garden of Forking Paths

The Faustus of the chapbook, or Marlowe's Faustus, signs an agreement with the devil according to the following simple plan: you gratify my desires for a period of time, I'll give you my soul. But Goethe modifies this bargain considerably: his Faust has an open-ended contract, to be terminated not after a set number of years, but only at the moment when Faust is at last satisfied: you can drag me off in chains as soon as I say to the passing moment, "Linger yet, thou art so fair!" (l. 1700). Time stand still here!—Faust is betting that his capacity for desire exceeds any fulfillment that Mephistopheles can offer. Whatever Mephistopheles provides, Faust (he thinks) will want more. He is wagering on his own creative power, his ability to invent ever newer, ever more clever and recondite desires. Faust understands himself as a genius of lacking, a sack that gets emptier the more it is filled, a reverse cornucopia, the rhapsode of the void. Faust is himself a spirit that denies: he conducts such a thorough devaluation of things that total possession of the universe is insufficient to still his restless longings. Mephistopheles embodies not only Faust's imagination, but also his capacity to say no. Faust has overwhelming pride in his power to be bored.

Goethe's structure for the poem exactly follows the growing intricacy of Faust's desires, his evolution into increasingly sophisticated and abnormal patterns of wishing. Faust's initial requests are fairly commonplace, in the manner of the older Faustuses: get me some booze, make me feel young again, get me a woman. But even these commonplace desires involve Faust in a strange attenuation of outer reality: as the world twists itself into an accommodating shape, it loses solidity. In the scene at Auerbach's tavern, Mephistopheles drills holes into the wood at the edge of the table, out of which there gush wines; but when a carouser lets some of the wine spill on the floor, it instantly flashes up as fire (l. 2300); the whole setting grows drunken and queasy, incoherent, as desire molds it into a locus of fantastic hope and fear. The actual tavern has started to thaw into the sort of place described by the spirits that sang Faust to sleep just before the signing of the contract—the dream-place where grapes endlessly fall into the hopper of the winepress, and plunge down in torrents of foaming wine, drop through the clean stones of the high places, broaden into great seas (l. 1481). Walt Disney's artists—who often appealed to Goethe for inspiration—used this song as the basis of an episode in *Fantasia* (1940), set to the music of

Beethoven's Sixth Symphony; and in a sense Goethe's *Faust* is less a stage piece than a prefiguration of an animated cartoon, where gravity and all physical laws are arbitrary, and it is so if you think so.

Critics have often noted that some of the scenes defy theatrical interpretation altogether—for obvious reasons, in the case of the stage direction "*A seven-league boot sidles up. Another quickly follows. Mephistopheles climbs down. The boots stride quickly away*" (l. 10066), which would puzzle George Lucas's special-effects shop, let alone a German stage director in the early nineteenth century. But even some of the simpler scenes, such as the scene before the gate, describe action difficult to realize on stage: peasants and townsmen sing and dance and flirt; eventually Faust and Wagner stroll far away from the revelers and at last come to a high place, where Faust sees a black poodle spiraling round him with rings of fire (l. 1154). The action is at once too diffuse and fluid, and too piecemeal: it appeals to a mental theatre, a wish-theatre,[9] where action can continue beyond the limits of any proscenium arch, and where hiatuses in the action are not felt as assaults on logic, but only as areas of the plot not yet imagined.

Goethe referred to *Faust* as a *Schwammfamilie,* a term that might be translated as a sponge colony.[10] I don't know whether Goethe knew that a live sponge, if forced through a wire mesh, will reconstitute itself on the other side, as if nothing had happened; but in any case Goethe's poem shows the same capacity for groping toward soft-edged loose shapes. Goethe wrote the poem spongewise, by writing one scene, then another scene at a completely different point in the story, and then (perhaps decades later) a third scene to fill in the gap. But—except for the Gretchen sections—the scenes rarely feel smoothly joined, consequential: we leap from Auerbach's tavern to the witch's kitchen (where Faust gets the drug that rejuvenates him) to the town street where Faust sees Gretchen, without any explanation or transition to cover these abruptions. According to Kafka, the Great Wall of China was built simultaneously over its whole length, in short sections, which the laborers struggled incessantly to connect;[11] Goethe's *Faust* was constructed according to exactly the same principle, a sort of inspired fumbling toward an integrity it could never quite achieve. Just as Faust's imagination leads to a general deliquescing of things, so Goethe's imagination is a sort of stream on which there bob bits of text. Nietzsche called Wagner a miniaturist;[12] and so is Goethe, even in a poem of 12,111 lines.

The poem is at once a set of fragments and a palimpsest. At one point Goethe shows Faust reading Luther's Bible—Luther was an exact contemporary of the historical Johannes Faust—in a state of dissatisfaction: he doesn't like the line *In the beginning was the Word,* so he crosses out the word *Word* and experiments with substitute nouns—*Thought? Strength?*— until finally he hits upon a line he likes: *In the beginning was the Deed* (l. 1237). We may feel that Goethe's poem is also continually erasing itself, testing alternative constructions of itself. The poem is a succession of novelties, in the manner of a circus, not a steady prosecution of a linear theme. Indeed all of Part Two is a sort of mischievous overwriting of Part One, in which Goethe provides a classical Walpurgisnight instead of a witches' sabbath, and a classical heroine—Helena—instead of Gretchen. Every reader who begins Part Two is disconcerted by the fact that Gretchen not only is forgotten, but also seems (almost) never to have existed at all: Part Two is a radical reconstruction of the Faust material, in a bizarrely independent manner, as if Part One were suspended or superseded, temporarily invalidated, made unwritten. These oddities of construction are Goethe's way of showing his own Faustian excess of imagination: instead of provided a drama with a causal chain, obeying the classical unities of time, place, and action, Goethe provides a plot that is pure deviation, a garden of forking paths, in which the place jumps at random from Leipzig to the Pharsalian Fields, in which the time jumps at random from the Renaissance to antiquity to the Middle Ages, in which the protagonist is at once old and young, murderer and wholly innocent. So forked is Faust's path that he can find himself in two or more places at the same time, lying in a coma in Wagner's laboratory while disporting among Leda and her attendants bathing in a crystal brook (l. 6916)—and soon Wagner and Mephistopheles will plunge into the same myth. Faust is a bilocated and imbricated thing, leading several lives at the same time, effortlessly sloughing off worn-out versions of himself, without any core predicate of identity. When Faust renounces his books, at the beginning of the poem, he dehistoricizes himself, unselves himself, embarks on a disjointed and inconsistent, poly-pneumatic career, or set of careers, as if he were caught in an avant-garde cinema, absurdly spliced together from bits and pieces of *The Raiders of the Lost Ark*, *Goodbye Mr. Chips*, *Svengali*, and *Clash of the Titans*. He is a human hypertext.

4. A Real Girl

In a number of ways, Goethe's poem confesses that there is something desperately wrong about Faust's mode of being, as he moves further and further into the apprehension of his desire, into the valley of his making. In the manner of cartoon characters, he confidently walks off the edge of the cliff, and is supported by thin air until he takes the trouble to look down.

Faust's first desire was to join the drinkers in Auerbach's tavern. His second desire is to drink a magic potion, to restore him to youth—to cast off most of his eighty years. To achieve this, Mephistopheles takes Faust to the witch's kitchen. This scene owes little to earlier accounts of the Faust legend: it is one of Goethe's most original inventions. The witch's kitchen is full of witch's kitsch, including a fine big cauldron right out of *Macbeth*, a magic mirror, a family of monkeys, and a large ball—the male monkey explains, while rolling the ball on the floor,

> The world is this ball,
> see it rise, fall,
> roll over, roll over:
> it clinks like glass—
> a breakable mass—
> inside all hollow. (ll. 2402–7)

Why a monkey, a mirror, and a globe?—because the witch's kitchen is a domain of hollow images. To *ape* is to imitate foolishly; to *mirror* is to reflect a likeness on a film of metal-backed glass; and to *map* is project the contours of a region, in much diminished scale, onto a flat piece of paper or a sphere. In every way Goethe is trying to show that Faust is surrounded by eidola, by empty phantoms of delight; and by drinking the witch's potion Faust is thinning himself into two dimensions, turning into an image on a mirror or a crystal ball, a monstrously distorted convex thing. The normal world may or may not be, as the monkey says, a hollow sphere of glass, easily broken; but the witchy world that Faust now enters is certainly just such a realm. Faust is choosing to dwell on a soap bubble, transformed into a man miraculously young and peppy, sexually irresistible. But these new traits are valid only, so to speak, in a space created by computer graphics, a virtual space subject to every sort of idle and whimsical change. Here the pilot may crash into a mountain and see his own legs and arms, as well as pieces of the fuselage, scatter wildly in all directions; but he has only to punch the restart button, and the crash never happened at all.

Faust, of course, can't accept the purely imagistic and illusory character of his experience, of himself. Marlowe's Faustus was, for the most part, content to manipulate shadows, to be a sixteenth-century peep-show operator; but Goethe's Faust demands that his illusions simultaneously retain their illusoriness (their power of being switched on and off, magnifying or diminishing at will) and yet be real. In order to cultivate himself, in order to take to heart all human pleasure and pain, in order to shipwreck himself through overintensities of feeling (l. 1775), Faust must convince himself of the authenticity of his experience. This demand for actuality is what ruins Gretchen's life—the helpless harmless girl is led to poison her mother and drown her illegitimate daughter; but it weakens considerably in Part Two of the poem, as Faust slowly learns to delight in the non-actual—in virtuality, in pantomime, in pattern-for-pattern's sake. Part Two begins with Mephistopheles' invention of paper money—that is, virtual money instead of real gold—and continues through a variety of exciting charades, as when the troops of the rival emperor thrash about on dry land, because they imagine that they are drowning in a flood (l. 10740). But in the second half of Part One, the Gretchen tragedy, Faust refuses to accept that there is anything feigned or factitious about Gretchen, or their love, or himself. And yet, a girl who was first beheld as a "heavenly image" in a witch's magic mirror (l. 2429) may well retain a certain pictorial character, a certain thinness of being. The tragedy of the Gretchen episode lies in the incapacity of Faust to believe in the lies that he tells himself about his love for Gretchen, and in the incapacity of Gretchen to become credible. She wants to be a real girl, but, unlike Pinocchio, she remains a "puppet"—to use Mephistopheles' and Faust's not wholly endearing term for her (ll. 2651, 3476).

Goethe tried hard to make Gretchen charming, and even, to some degree, psychologically complex: he provided her with a scene in which she learns compassion for an unmarried pregnant girl, formerly the object of her scorn; with scenes of solitary desolation, both in a song and in an anguished prayer before the image of the Virgin Mary; with a scene in the Cathedral where an evil spirit troubles her conscience, until she faints while the choir chants the *Dies irae*; and with a scene in prison, extraordinary in its pathetic irony, where the mad Gretchen mistakes Faust for her executioner. But I believe that *Faust* is essentially a monodrama, and that Goethe is participating in Faust's own plan to discover persuasive evidence that Gretchen is an actual human being, and not a slightly trite picture of innocence waiting to be wronged, or an allegory of defenseless chastity. Jane K. Brown traces the character of Gretchen back to the stereotyped victims of seduction in English restoration dramas, such as Calista in Nicholas Rowe's *Fair Penitent* (1703).[13] And Gretchen so thoroughly exposes the clichéd nature of Faust's sexual desire that she pulls the whole poem back into melodrama.

In the Gretchen scenes—among the earliest parts of the poem to be written—Goethe is at his most dramatic, as opposed to epical or lyrical or fantastical or satirical: we find ourselves confronted with something like a well-made play, in which the behavior of the characters in one scene is a consequence of the behavior of the characters in the previous scene—far from Goethe's normal rhythm of erasure and new bewonderment. But neither Faust nor Gretchen ever masters the art of being a character in a well-made seduction drama:

> *Margarete.* Do you believe in God?
> *Faust.* Dear girl, who dares affirm it:
> "I believe in God"?
> Go ask a priest, go ask a hermit,
> and their response will seem to mock
> the girl who asks the question.
> *Margarete.* You don't believe?
> *Faust.* Oh, don't misunderstand, my darling love!

Who can name it,
who proclaim it,
"I believe in him"—
who can feel it,
who dare reveal it,
"I don't believe in him"?
          The all-comprehender,
the all-preserver,
doesn't he clasp and cherish
you, me, himself? . . .
          Fill your heart, your heart is big enough!
And when your heart is wholly full of love,
name it whatever you like!
Name it luck! Heart! Love! God!
I don't have a name
for it! Feeling is everything,—
name is sound and smoke,
cloud over the high fire.
Margarete. I like hearing you say those words.
As pretty as what the pastor says,
though *his* terms are a little different. (ll. 3426–41, 3451–61)

In a seduction play, the male lead would here be spouting deliberate malarkey, with no intention except to make the girl swoon in his arms. And indeed Mephistopheles understands scenes such as this one exactly in the terms of a seduction play: he mocks Faust for "feeling inside all six days of creation," and notes that Faust's mighty raptures culminate in a sensation that can't be described in words, only indicated by an obscene gesture (ll. 3287, 3291).

But the Gretchen tragedy isn't quite a seduction play. The speech doesn't exist for the sake of wooing the girl; instead, the girl exists for the sake of eliciting the speech, for admiring the speech, for enabling Faust's rhetorical gifts to shine. Faust and Gretchen began their intimacy with a little scene in which Gretchen plucked a daisy, and pulled off its petals one by one, saying, "He loves me—loves me not" (l. 3181); and now, as their intimacy nears its climax, they play another game, "He believes in God—believes not in God." Both these games concern authenticity of feeling—dangerous pastimes, for if authenticity is a function of a word game, it is surely unattainable. Goethe's Faust wants, above all, to be a poet—his whole bargain with Mephistopheles exists for the sake of rousing him to brilliant peaks of feeling, for giving him matter for wild excursions of discourse into the ineffable. Mephistopheles will, later, provide a delirious vision of classical antiquity to enable Faust to be a new Ovid; but here Faust is given a Barbie doll, less for the sake of seduction than for the sake of fooling around with the rhetoric of seduction, for the sake of tossing around various scarves and panaches from the wardrobe of Don Juan. (It was scarcely necessary for Grabbe to write his *Don Juan und Faust*—Goethe had already experimented with that synthesis.) When the doll's dress gets torn, and its head pops off, Faust will throw her aside, and she scarcely will have existed at all. I overstate the purely imagistic character of Gretchen in order to counteract the pathos that her plight inevitably, and properly, generates in the reader: Goethe is playing his own game in the liminal regions between authenticity and inauthenticity, sometimes allowing Gretchen to complexify into an empathizable subject, at other times dismissing her as a hollow object of desire, with a limited range of movement in her arms and legs, and for all her compliancy brittle and easily broken.

5. Wall-purging

As Part One of *Faust* approaches its end, all illusion of heft and solidness and authenticity breaks down, and Faust enters a world of sheer madness, hallucination. When his desire was limited to attainable things, such as wine, a town girl, a stimulant beverage, and an anti-wrinkle cream, Faust could recognize both himself and his surroundings; but as he strides farther into the domain of wanting, he and his environment start to grow really strange. W. H. Auden—who once called himself "a minor atlantic Goethe"[14] and who remains a good guide to the pathologies of imagination in which Goethe specialized—made a distinction between desires and wishes. A desire is real when there exists a possibility for fulfilling it; a desire is unreal—a wish—when there is no such possibility. If an American businessman wants a Cadillac, and can't have one, a definite reason can always be given; but "if the Chinese peasant asks, 'Why cannot I buy a Cadillac?' there are an infinite number of reasons which can only be summed up in the quite irrational answer, 'Because I am I.' "[15]

After seducing Gretchen, Faust's desires are basically spent; for most of the rest of the poem he will concentrate on wishes. Why can't I waltz with a witch on the summit of the Brocken? Why can't I conjure up Greek demigods to fondle one another for general amusement? Why can't I frolic with mermaids by the shores of the Aegean? Why won't Helen of Troy sleep with me and bear my child? For me, there are an infinite number of reasons that patiently explain the frustration of these wishes. But for Faust, living in an artificial domain of frustrationlessness, it is easy to accomplish all these things, and more. Because he no longer possesses a distinct *I*, the restriction *Because I am I* no longer obtains: as Faust mutates into various figments of his own wishes, he becomes increasingly adept at feeling at home in any plane of fantasy he chooses to enter. There is always an element of self-contradictoriness in wishing, as a diary entry of Brecht's makes clear: "Of course I want Timbuktu and a child and a house and no doors and to be alone in bed and to have a woman in bed, the apple off the tree and the timber too, and not to wield the axe and to have the tree complete with blossom, apples, and foliage."[16] But Faust, unlike Brecht, is in the happy position that one wish doesn't exclude any other wish—a stroll down one path doesn't prevent a stroll down another path, in a different direction. Faust can eat his cake and have it too, for deprivation is a consequence, and Faust has managed to find himself in a completely inconsequential world.

This is not to say that the wish-world is necessarily a happy place. Faust learns that gratification can be condition of terror, for we discover things we don't like about ourselves when we find out exactly what we want. Again the example of that belated Faustian Kurtz, in Conrad's *Heart of Darkness,* is relevant: Kurtz enters the Congo and assumes god-like authority over the natives for the noblest goal, for the sake of bringing enlightenment to the savage peoples; but he winds up as a bloodthirsty tyrant, bawling for general extermination of the Africans. Goethe's Faust also beholds something of the monstrousness of his own appetites, in the Walpurgisnight revels. There is a character in the Walpurgisnight, based on the author and critic Friedrich Nicolai, who wrote a parody of Goethe's novel *The Sorrows of Young Werther,* ridiculing Goethe for his sentimental excesses; but in later life the rationalist Nicolai was prey to hallucinations, which he hoped to cure by applying leeches to his buttocks. Goethe refers to him as the Proktophantasmist (l. 4144), the Man who Dreams with his Anus. And indeed the Walpurgisnight really is an anal fantasy, full of witch-farts (l. 3961), goats, and other bad smells. It is also a penile fantasy, as we note when Faust dances with a young witch who teases him with her breast-apples (l. 4132), and Mephistopheles, dancing with an old witch, tells her his dream of a hole in the split trunk of a tree (l. 4137). When Faust dreams, he dreams with his whole body: the Walpurgisnight is a pan-sexual carnival in which anus and penis speak, in which a witch's mouth may emit a word in the form of a little red mouse (l. 4179), in which Goethe gives vent to personal spite against his enemies, for all the normal boundaries of discourse are vanishing, even the boundary between character and author.

The Walpurgisnight presents a fully animist landscape, in which the whole locale is a great trembling body, sensitive to, interpenetrating with, the bodies of the characters who move on it, through it. The split tree is at once a coarse figure of speech and an element of the scenery; and, as Faust, Mephistopheles, and the Will-of-the-Wisp make their way, they stumble through a bizarrely flickering terrain, decomposed and deliquesced, in which earth and air and fire and water are all balled up into a locus of nightmare:

And like snakes the groping roots
curl themselves from sand and rock,

stretch out queerly from the muck,
frighten us and snare our foot.
Knot-holes thrust out after us
arms just like an octopus . . . (ll. 3894–99)

Here is the exact verbal equivalent of Wölfflin's vision of German art: a
unitary field in which the human figures and their surroundings are wavering expressions of the same lines of force. Faust wanders through a landscape that is simply a magnified image of his terror and his horniness, a
landscape generated by the relaxation of all the mind's and body's sphinc-
ters.

In this sheerly unsuppressed place, nothing can be held back, everything
must appear: and so the haunting image of Gretchen must take its place
with all the other images of scary or forbidden wishings:

Faust.   Mephisto, can you see
that pale and pretty child, alone and loitering there? . . .
Mephistopheles. Don't look at her! A harmful thing to see,
a lifeless idol, thing of sorcery.
To meet with her is never good:
her frozen gaze can freeze your human blood,
and turn you to a man of stone . . .
Medusa has that look, alone!
Faust. You're right, those are a corpse's eyes,
never closed by any loving finger!
That is the breast that Gretchen let me kiss,
that is the body where my hands once lingered!
Mephistopheles. You fool avid for folly, you never get enough!
She always takes the shape of a man's best love.
Faust. What immense sorrow! And what joy!
From her still gaze I—cannot turn away.
How strange, how strange—a little strip of red
encircles like a necklace her white neck,
a line as thin as a knife's back! (ll. 4183–84, 4189–4205)

In this clairvoyance of a Gretchen already beheaded for her crimes, Faust
trespasses on forbidden ground: his imagination has come upon an image
so powerful, so accusatory, that it threatens to paralyze his whole creative
faculty, to bring to a halt those wildly careering motions of willfulness that
have guided him so far. A man who predicates his whole self on wishing is
in a perilous state if the wishing were to stop: he may collapse into a state
of nullity, for extremes tend to converge, and being everything is much like
being nothing. The last wish is the wish to be rid of wishes: not just to be
dead, but never to have been a desirous subject at all.

When Goethe first published a more-or-less complete Part One of *Faust,* in 1808, there was a swift trajectory of despair from the vision of Gretchen at the end of the Walpurgisnight scene to Faust's great final cry "I wish I had never been born" (l. 4596)—after Gretchen insists she must go to her death, instead of escaping from jail. But for the 1826 republication, Goethe softened the effect by inserting an intermezzo, *Walpurgisnight-dream, or the Golden Wedding of Oberon and Titania,* after the Walpurgisnight scene. In this extremely self-conscious and artificial ballad, various characters from Shakespeare—Oberon, Puck, Ariel—mingle with witches and idealists and realists and dogmatics and skeptics and other metaphysically challenged masks, amid much plinking and tooting and chirruping from the orchestra. The theatre here calls attention to its theatricality: instead of psychological intensities, instead of immersion inside a defeated and indefeasible sensibility, we have jests and japes, clowning and spoofing. Goethe here foreshadows the method of Part Two: if Part One offers a desperate engrossment in desire and wish, Part Two will devise a relief from desire and wish. And this relief is achieved by an appeal to Shakespeare—to Oberon and Titania, but most of all to Ariel.

6. Fairy Optics

Shakespeare has sometimes been criticized for trivializing the fairies. In the old Germanic and Celtic myths, the fairies are pagan gods, full of terror; but Shakespeare liked his fairies small and cute, tucked adorably in a cowslip bell, or riding merrily on a bat's back. In the old stories the fairies mutilate animals and kidnap children for abominable rites; in Shakespeare, a fairy's idea of a good joke is to spoil a tub of butter, or to play tricks with novelty items along the lines of dribble glasses and whoopee cushions.[17] Part Two of *Faust* has often displeased readers—especially readers who want more pathos along the lines of the Gretchen tragedy—because of its levity, its frivolousness, its sprawl, its contrived and mannered wit. But Goethe understood that the only sequel to Part One could be an entry into a domain of pure playfulness, where nothing much is at stake—and for this domain Shakespeare's fairies are the right muses.

In Part One Faust craved all sorts of intense and overwhelming sensations; but these sensations didn't provide the dilation of being for which he'd hoped, so in Part Two he wants entertainment. He isn't cured of wishing, but his wishes now aren't so deeply rousing, so deeply involved in his sympathetic nervous system. He is now content with a more cerebral sort of elation; the creatures of his fantasy, while often grotesque, tend to be amusing, not horrifying. So it is appropriate that the first speech of Part Two is a song accompanied by an Aeolian harp, sung by Ariel, who induces Faust to a region of general amenity and oblivion. In Part One there

was too much dark, too much feeling; but in Part Two, the sun rises, and
the newly awakened Faust turns his gaze away from the sun, toward the
lovely rainbow glimpsed in a waterfall: "In refractions of color our lives
take place" (l. 4727), Faust meditates, as he enters the omniform, gaudy
world of his new life. Goethe considered himself a scientist specializing in
optics, and argued, against Newton, that white light was a primary phenomenon (not merely a confused mixture of colors), and that color arose
from the interaction of white light with the material world. In Part Two
Faust's mind is a sort of giant prism, teasing out of white light a wide
assortment of amazing shapes and colors—griffins and sphinxes and talking ants—in the manner of a magic lantern show. When Homunculus—a
little artificial man whom Wagner crystallizes in a glass retort (l. 6860)—
appears on the scene, the poem confesses its essentially vitreous and specular character. There was always a certain Disneyworld aspect to Faust's
domain of wishing; but in Part Two that aspect will be increasingly explicit, as Faust discovers how to confect painless fantasy-scapes, in which
the wind is itself music, and all the clouds are made of nitrous oxide. Ariel
increasingly infiltrates the role of Mephistopheles, who starts to become a fairy of sweet dreams; inside those dreams he plays the scape-
grace buffoon whose bellowings provide comic relief—Mephistopheles
as Falstaff.

There is a new artfulness to Faust's wishes. In the *Critique of Judgment*
(1790), Kant argues that the pleasure in seeing, say, the Mona Lisa differs
from the pleasure of eating a good steak, in that the delight that dwells in
the contemplation of the picture isn't the result of satisfying a specific appetite: aesthetic pleasure is disinterested pleasure, not grounded on pre-
existent need. Faust, in Part Two, steps hesitantly into the realm of aesthetics, where the joy of beholding forms depends less and less on desires for
food, drink, and sex, or for floods of intense sensation, and more and more
on purely ocular voluptuousness. The strenuous desiring and wishing of
Part One yields to a state of delicate velleity; the jagged images of Part One,
attesting to ferocities of will, vanish, and Faust attends to a succession of
images that are not only inconsequent, but which give deliberate pleasure
through their inconsequence, as if a lecturer on the history of art mixed up
slides from all different times and places, and stimulated his audience
through the smiling incongruities.

7. Traveling South

Goethe's *Faust* is a book intimately bound up with art history. In 1867 the
young Walter Pater published an essay on the art historian Johann Joachim
Winckelmann, which made large claims concerning Winckelmann's influence on Goethe's *Faust*:

... that note of revolt against the eighteenth century, which we detect in
Goethe, was struck by Winckelmann. Goethe illustrates a union of the
Romantic spirit, in its adventure, its variety, its profound subjectivity of
soul, with Hellenism, in its transparency, its rationality, its desire of
beauty—that marriage of Faust and Helena, of which the art of the nineteenth century is the child, the beautiful lad Euphorion, as Goethe con-
ceives him, on the crags in the "splendour of battle and in harness as for
victory" [*Faust,* l. 9853], his brows bound with light.[18]

Goethe never met Winckelmann—Winckelmann was murdered by a thief
on the road home from Italy, just as Goethe was planning to meet him—
but Goethe revered him as an instinctive pagan, whose learned and detailed celebration of the beauty of classical antiquity (serene, disciplined,
ideal) helped to widen the culture of Europe. To Goethe, Greece and Rome
were made visible to the modern sensibility through Winckelmann's eyes;
and when Goethe considered what it meant to a Northern genius (such as
Faust—or Goethe), he constructed his model by contrast with the Southern genius, as presented by the writings of Winckelmann. And Pater was
right in believing that Goethe—with his tremendous resources of synthetic
imagination—hoped to achieve a fusion of North (the obscure and deep)
and South (the right-proportioned and lucid).

   Indeed, Goethe's marriage of Faust and Helena has determined part of the
major curriculum for art history to the present day. Pater's *The Renaissance* is
itself an attempt to marry the North and the South: Pater everywhere contrasts Northern psychological subtlety with Southern aesthetic stasis:

> *Allgemeinheit*—breadth, generality, universality—is the word chosen
> by Winckelmann, and after him by Goethe and many German critics, to
> express that law of the most excellent Greek sculptors, of Pheidias and
> his pupils, which prompted them constantly to seek the type in the indi-
> vidual, to abstract and express only what is structural and permanent,
> to purge from the individual all that belongs only to him, all the acci-
> dents, the feelings and actions of the special moment . . . the Greek way
> . . . involved to a certain extent the sacrifice of what we call *expression*.[19]

Occasionally Pater saw transient nuances in Southern art—for instance in
the sculpture of the della Robbias, in which "The whole essence of their
work is *expression,* the passion of a smile over the face of a child, the ripple
of the air on a still day over the curtain of a window jar";[20] but mostly
Pater found such things in Northern art, in Goethe and Victor Hugo, and
especially in Browning—"what a cobweb of allusions, what double and
treble reflexions of the mind upon itself, what an artificial light is constructed and broken."[21] And, at the end of the Winckelmann essay, Pater
aligns his own preferences with this Northern sort of art:

For us, necessity is not, as of old, a sort of mythological personage without us, with whom we can do warfare. It is rather a magic web woven through and through us, like that magnetic system of which modern science speaks, penetrating us with a network, subtler than our subtlest nerves, yet bearing in it the central forces of the world.[22]

Southern art is the domain of fixed images; Northern art is the domain of fields of force. Southern art is palpable and detached; Northern art is elusive, a nimbus that flickers between the nervous system of the spectator and the contemplated object.

Similar models of North and South can be found in more recent art history. As we've seen, Heinrich Wölfflin presents the identical mythology of North and South: his book on Italy and the German feeling for form seems to follow exactly from Pater and Winckelmann. Indeed Wölfflin seems to be actualizing intellectual potentials embedded deeply in Goethe's *Faust.*

Part Two of *Faust* is an optical game, in which Faust recedes from and draws near the images generated by his imagination. As he pulls away into detached contemplation—watching the Classical Walpurgisnight without taking part in the action—he experiments with a Winckelmannian, essentially Southern attitude toward art: the beholding sensibility grows tenuous, impersonal, and the images become distinct and isolated. He can even woo Helena in cool and poised verse, as if he were marrying a statue; and their child, Euphorion (whose career is based on that of Lord Byron), seems begotten not in a passionate spasm, but as an act of frigid allegorification—as Goethe said, "Euphorion . . . is not a human, but an allegorical being. In him is personified poetry; which is bound to neither time nor place nor person."[23] Two other passages from the *Conversations with Eckermann* suggest how Goethe consciously sharpened his imagistic focus in Part Two—how the emphasis shifts from the thick, turbid, brooding sensibility of Faust to the lucid acuities of separate images:

"The first part is almost entirely subjective; it proceeded entirely from a perplexed impassioned individual, and his semi-darkness is probably highly pleasing to mankind. But in the second part there is scarcely anything of the subjective; here is seen a higher, broader, clearer, more passionless world. . . ."[24]

"The old Walpurgis Night," said Goethe, "is monarchical, since the devil is there respected throughout as a decided chief. But the classic Walpurgis Night is thoroughly republican, since all stand on a plain near one another, so that each is as prominent as his associates, and nobody is subordinate or troubled about the rest."

"Moreover," said I, "in the classic assembly all are sharply outlined individualities; while, on the German Blocksberg, each individuality is lost in the general witch-mass."[25]

It is remarkable, how strongly both Goethe and his friend Eckermann seem to understand the dialectic of the poem in pictorial terms, as a tension between a method of bold outlines and a method of shadowy chiaroscuro.

And yet, Eckermann here exaggerates the distinctness of the images of Part Two. The tendency of the distinct images to retreat toward the horizon, to insist on their immiscible isolation, is strong; but there is also a certain counter-tendency to smear these images into a general puddle. The classical Walpurgisnight ends in a hymn to Eros, as Homunculus shatters his glass carapace and quenches his vivid spark in the ocean—he sublimes out of individuality into the state of being a creative germ, a light that transfigures the waves (l. 8474). The images undo themselves—again, the imagination shows itself at last as a faculty that dissolves, diffuses, dissipates.

8. Rhymes and Similes

Even on the level of language, Part Two shows a certain tension between Southern precision and Northern dissipation and energy. There are passages that so strongly imitate classical syntax that Goethe's German sounds like half-translated Greek or Latin: negligent of normal word order, as if each word were a separate bead capable of being arranged in the sentence in any sequence at all. It isn't easy to give in English—a language poor in case endings—an impression of these daringly classicized German hexameters:

> Into the shuddering ritual of this night, as often
> before, step forth I, Erichtho, I, the dark one;
> less abomination than the hurtful poets say . . .
>   No one gladly grants dominion to another,
> no one gladly grants it to him who won it by force
> and forcefully lords it. For everyone who knows not
> how to rule himself, rules with too much pleasure
> his neighbor's will, according to his arrogant intent. (ll. 7005–7,
>   7013–17)

The tremendous exactness of the placement of the words, the tight knots of riddling syntax, all suggest the Southern mind, distinguished and distinguishing, captious, carefully qualified. But there is also a Northern style of poetry, which puzzles Helen of Troy in one of the most memorable passages of the Helena episode:

> *Lynceus.* Already see the army tame,
> all their swords are blunt and lame,
> before that noble splendid form
> the sun itself seems dull, unwarm,

and from that face a glory falls
that makes all empty, and all null. . . .
Helena. Many wonders I see, and many hear.
Amazement strikes, questions come to mind.
But first I wish instruction, why this man's speech
rings so strange, amiable and yet so strange.
One sound, it seems, conforms itself to others,
and if a word is conjoined to the ear,
another comes, sweetly to fondle the first. (ll. 9350–55, 9365–71)

Helen of Troy, being a classical Greek, has never before heard rhymed verse—an invention of the barbarous North—and is charmed, bewildered by the chiming sounds. A poetry made of echoes is equivalent to a painting style of blurry fields, in the manner described by Wölfflin: instead of brilliantly pointed and logically inflected single words, we have a chant, an incantation, an effect of general verbal mass.

Few poets would allow a love scene between Faust and Helena to turn into an verse essay in criticism, in the manner of Boileau or Alexander Pope, concerning the history of rhyme in Western poetry. We feel that we should be attending to the subject matter; but instead, Goethe asks us to attend to the style, to the verbal surface. In Part Two, the artificiality of art continually calls attention to itself—on the levels of painting, music, and poetry itself. The descriptive power of the language stiffens until, in the final scene, Goethe seems to be painting an imaginary Coreggio-like fresco of the Adoration of the Virgin; and musical cues start to pop up on a regular basis—Goethe provides such stage directions as "*Tumult of war in the orchestra, finally changing into cheerful military tunes*" (l. 10782). Part One was subjective in that all sensory phenomena were ultimately referred to the sensorium of Faust; but in the more objective Part Two, all sensory phenomena are elevated into a finical aesthetic dignity. There was even a unique passage of prose in Part One, called *Dismal Day,* just after the Walpurgisnight-dream, in which Faust's misery reached such a pitch of intensity that he could no longer speak verse at all; by contrast, in Part Two, Faust seems more interested in talking about assonance and consonance than in talking about wild love. Even in his dejection, the Faust of Part Two is astonishingly attentive to the rhyme-structure of his discourse:

Four came in, but only three went out;
the sense of their words left me in doubt.
A sound dying away, something like *breath,*
a fearful rhyme-word followed: *death.* (ll. 11398–401)

(The German rhyme-words are *Not* and *Tod,* need and death.) Throughout Part One, Faust craved a poet's imaginative power; but now the poet is vanishing into the poem. Part One was a study of plot and character; Part Two is a study in diction, illustration, and verbal music—*lexis, opsis,* and *melos,* to use Aristotle's terms for the parts of a tragedy.

As Faust confesses his status as a character in a rhyming poem, we seem to be given an unusually intimate glimpse of Goethe in the poet's workshop, musing over the texture of his verse. In *Der westöstliche Diwan*— concerning a love affair between an elderly Oriental poet named Hatem and a young woman, a situation that faintly disguises autobiography— Goethe rhymes *Morgenröte* (dawn) with *Hatem,* an outrageous violation of protocol, but forgivable in that the poet expects the reader to note the discord and to substitute for *Hatem* the name that works as a rhyme, *Goethe.* In Part Two of *Faust,* similarly, every outbreak of meta-poetry brings us closer to Goethe, further from Faust.

The demotion of Faust in Part Two can be felt in many ways. In the Prologue to Part One—the debate between God and Mephistopheles concerning Faust's temptability—God gave Mephistopheles permission to lead Faust into any error whatsoever—"As long as he strives, a man will err" (l. 317). God believes—and who is in a position to contradict him?—that any path, no matter how devious, will turn out to be the right path, if it is followed vigorously. As Blake puts the matter in a contemporary work, *The Marriage of Heaven and Hell* (1793), "If the fool would persist in his folly he would become wise."[26] And indeed, by the end of Part Two, Faust seems to have found the right path: all his furies of wishing and willing and striving have become channeled into a project to drain swamps, to reclaim arable land from the sea. In Part One there were far too many Fausts; in Part Two, his lurching, volatile, incoherent sensibility settles into a fairly simple mask of ethical rectitude, but loses most of its energy in the process. The poem's dynamic shifts away from the character of Faust, as the name "Faust" becomes a mere pretext for dazzling textual feats—the verse preens in its own elegance and power, in the absence of any real subject matter.

In the end Mephistopheles wins the wager, for Faust, wholly tuckered out, says Linger! to the passing moment (l. 11582), and dies; but Mephistopheles loses Faust's soul, for when he tries to collect it, he must shrink back, for angels pelt him with roses, roses that burn him worse than the fires of hell (l. 11755). In the famous final scene of Part Two, Faust dwindles to zero—he, or his soul, is silent during the scene—and yet manages a sort of chromatic saturation, distaining the fields of heaven with his Faustness. The Blessed Boys, weaving circles in the sky, appoint Faust as their new instructor: "For this one is learned, / let *him* be our teacher" (ll. 12082–83). The straying pedagogue has returned to the university: the professor has been called to a chair in heaven. But these Blessed Boys are not mere generic cherubs or putti, as Pater Seraphicus explains: they are the souls of miscarried fetuses, or children dead just after birth, with no workable brains or sense-organs—Pater Seraphicus has to invite them to enter his own celestial body, so that they can take part in the spectacle by availing themselves of *his* eyes and ears (l. 11906).

This is a bizarre fate for Faust, to become a sort of vicarious intelligence for the souls of the stillborn—and yet it is makes sense. One of the conspicuous characters of the last scene is *Una Poenitentium, once named Gretchen,* brought on stage to sing a hymn to the Virgin, in the same meter in which she prayed to the Virgin long ago, in Part One, for in heaven prosody is the chief badge of identification. And I believe that the host of the Blessed Boys must include the soul of the baby whom Gretchen drowned—Faust's own first child, who never lived at all, but is now endowed with the father's brilliance and breadth of life. The last scene of *Faust* is a sort of Heavenly Walpurgisnight, a mass of indistinct figures reveling in a blinding light, where Faust disperses into the radiation, becomes part of wisdom's sky. (The very first lines of the scene [ll. 11844–47], concerning a swaying forest and clutching roots, recall the Walpurgisnight of Part One.) On earth Faust investigated the whole horizon of experience, wherever wish and desire led him; in heaven all this experience is incorporated, made actual for those who knew little of earth. Heaven is enriched by Faust's inquiries into the far reaches of conation: Faust's fall—if he ever fell—is a fortunate one.

Faust spent the entire poem in search of something that is simultaneously stimulating and real; and he found a good deal of stimulation, but little reality. The heaven of the last scene is an allegation that there exists, beyond our world, a realm where aesthetic pleasure is absolute, where what is dreamed-of is real. In one of his most remarkable conversations, Goethe and Eckermann discussed a gorgeous painting by Rubens, in which the light came from two different directions at once, as if the sky contained two suns:

> "It is by this that Rubens proves himself great, and shows to the world that he, with a free spirit, stands *above* Nature, and treats her comformably to his high purposes. The double light is certainly a violent expedient, and you certainly say that it is contrary to Nature. But if it is contrary to Nature, I still say it is higher than Nature. It is the bold stroke of the master, by which he . . . proclaims to the world that his art is not entirely subject to natural necessities, but has laws of its own."[27]

Eckermann asked Goethe whether there was any phenomenon in literature comparable to Rubens' double light: Goethe replied that in *Macbeth* Lady Macbeth says she has given suck, whereas Macduff later notes that she never had children—and that Shakespeare happily rested in this contradiction, because he could not achieve the highest emphasis if he changed either of the speeches. In the domain of art, intensity is self-justifying.

Goethe composed his *Faust,* from beginning to end, according to the principle of double light—or triple, or *n*-fold. We've seen how consistently inconsistent the poem has been, as Goethe scratches out words, characters, whole scenic perspectives, in the frenzy of forward movement. By the end, the contradictions in Faust's character may seem resolved by his good works, his exhaustion, his death; but in some ways the contradictions are only increasing in the last scene, as Pater Profundus's voice from the depths chimes in with Pater Ecstaticus's voice from the heights, as the never-born commingle with the far-too-old. In heaven, opposites coexist amiably, with no jostling, no tension.

Most of *Faust* is a reeling through images that image other images; but the final scene tries to provide an image of something that is not an image, something actual. The Chorus Mysticus announces, in the very last lines of the poem, that the whole earth is nothing but a simile:

> Everything transient
> is merely a likeness;
> what's been insufficient,
> here becomes fullness;
> what cannot be written,
> here is done;
> the eternal-feminine
> pulls us on. (ll. 12104–11)

First the poem discussed the art of rhyming; now it discusses figures of speech, as it continues to haul itself up from content to form, from psychology to rhetoric, from will to representation, from signified to signifier. Behind this unforgettable chorus there lies the mirror of enigmas, from I Corinthians 13:12: "For now we see through a glass, darkly; but then face to face: now I know in part; but then shall know even as also I am known." Goethe is announcing that the poem is a gigantic convex glass, reflecting, with all sorts of funhouse distortions, certain truths beyond the range of thought and language, certain truths that can manifest themselves only through art. Plato taught that beauty is the splendor of truth, and the only ultimate that can be declared to the senses; and for Goethe, the increasingly frank confessions of artifice hint at his pride in an art not subservient to nature but beyond nature, an art that obeys no laws but its own, an art worthy of the supernatural. Rubens limited himself to a double light; Goethe's light, in the final scene of *Faust,* seems to come from all directions at once.

Faust died as a very old man, and the whole heavenscape of the last scene seems confected out of chaste and pious Italian frescoes. But it would be a mistake to think that *Faust* ends in a state of sexlessness, a condition beyond desire. The eternal-feminine that pulls us on suggests that heaven is instead an intensification of desire, a domain where perfect fulfillment simultaneously satisfies our thirst and increases it—that is, a domain that

extrapolates the hopeful earth on which Faust was so confident of his insa-
tiability that wagered his salvation on it. Sex—slightly sublimated, but
strangely overt—hovers everywhere in Goethe's heaven, so crammed with
ecstatic fathers penetrated by arrows (l. 11858), miscarried children, and
the souls of those whose bodies once gave such deep pleasure.
Mephistopheles, tormented by the burning roses, stares up at the cherubs
and is roused—masochist that he is—to sexual desire: "absurd and vulgar
lust attacks the devil— / protected as I am by hell's tar" (ll. 11838–39). In
the old Faustus stories, Mephistopheles fetched devils in women's clothes
to be Faustus's wife; but for Goethe the homosexuality latent in devils becomes explicit only on the very threshold of heaven. As we approach heaven,
we approach an omnisexual realm, where the blessed spirits are at once
nude and naked—at once cool poised forms, and erotic lures. If there is no
relief from appetite, it is simply because Goethe, the Romantic, cannot
comfortably imagine a state of joy disjunct from unappeasable desire. The
source of this desire, the object of this desire, is curiously abstract and
impersonal, not localized in a specific body but, seemingly, an attribute of
the whole heavenly region; but the desire is no less compulsive for that.
The eternal-feminine jerks us around.

From Goethe to Berlioz

1. Goethe in France

Faust departed from Germany in verse, but arrived in France in prose, in Nerval's widely admired translation,[1] in which there appear in verse only those passages that would be difficult to accept as prose, such as the song of the rat, the song of the flea, or the song about the king of Thule. Nerval's version was also incomplete, necessarily, since Goethe by 1828 hadn't yet finished the poem, even though he'd been working on it since the 1770s; in the event, Nerval didn't publish a translation of Part Two until 1840, after Goethe's death. Goethe wasn't at all troubled by the prosiness of Nerval's Part One, and told Eckermann that he was tremendously fond of Nerval's work: "I do not like . . . to read my *Faust* any more in German, but in this French translation all seems again fresh, new, and spirited . . . the first part is the product of a rather dark state in the individual."[2] It is not surprising that Nerval's translation would have reminded Goethe of the darkness of Part One, because the text feels darker in French than in German: partly because the use of prose removes from Goethe's subtle verbal patterning a level of formal artifice, contrivance, and finally hilarity. Berlioz, like many Frenchmen, knew Goethe's *Faust* only through Nerval's translation, and he read it as a black thing indeed.

Perhaps this feature can be illustrated by parallel passages from Goethe and Nerval:

Mephistopheles. Lass das nur stehn! Dabei wird's niemand wohl.
Es ist ein Zauberbild, ist leblos, ein Idol.
Ihm zu begegnen ist nicht gut:
vom starren Blick erstarrt des Menschen Blut,
und er wird fast in Stein verkehrt . . .
Von der Meduse hast du ja gehört!
Faust. Fürwahr, es sind die Augen eines Toten,
die einen liebende Hand nicht schloß!
Das ist die Brust, die Gretchen mir geboten,
das is der süße Leib, den ich genoß!

Mephistopheles. Das ist die Zauberei, du leicht verführter Tor!
Denn jedem kommt sie wie sein Liebchen vor. (ll. 4189–4200)

Mephistopheles. Don't look at her! A harmful thing to see,
a lifeless idol, thing of sorcery.
To meet with her is never good:
her frozen gaze can freeze your human blood,
and turn you to a man of stone . . .
Medusa has that look, alone!
Faust. You're right, those are a corpse's eyes,
never closed by any loving finger!
That is the breast that Gretchen let me kiss,
that is the body where my hands once lingered!
Mephistopheles. You fool avid for folly, you never get enough!
She always takes the shape of a man's best love.

Méphistophélès. Laisse cela! personne ne s'en trouve bien. C'est une figure magique, sans vie, une idole. Il n'est pas bon de la rencontrer; son regard fixe engourdit le sang de l'homme et le change presque en pierre. As-tu déjà entendu parler de la Méduse?
Faust. Ce sont vraiment les yeux d'un mort, qu'une main chérie n'a point fermés. C'est bien là le sein que Marguerite m'abandonna, c'est bien le corps si doux que je possédai!
Méphistophélès. C'est de la magie, pauvre fou, car chacun croit y retrouver celle qu'il aime.

Méphistophélès. Leave that alone!—it won't go well for you. It's a magic figure, lifeless, an idol. It is not good to meet her; her fixed stares numbs the blood of a man and almost turns him to stone. Have you ever heard of Medusa?
Faust. Those are truly the eyes of a corpse, that no cherished hand has ever closed. There's the breast that Marguerite abandoned to me, there's the sweet body that I possessed!
Méphistophélès. It's all magic, poor fool, for each man believes that he finds in her the woman he loves.

In prose, the passage seems remorseless, implacable; but in verse Faust and Mephistopheles seem on the verge of a dance. It is the difference between a ceremony of despair, and despair itself.

Nerval's verse, though extremely accomplished, also introduces alien tonalities into Goethe's text. Goethe's famous song for Gretchen at the spinning wheel sounds very different in Nerval:

Meine Ruh ist hin,
mein Herz ist schwer;
ich finde sie nimmer
und nimmermehr. (ll. 3374–77)

My heart sinks low,
my rest is gone;
I'll find it never,
never again.

Une amoureuse flamme
Consume mes beaux jours;
Ah! la paix de mon âme
A donc fui pour toujours!

In French, Gretchen seems languid, listless, nerveless; in German the clipped, two-beat lines seem edgy and anxious, as if her heartbeat were directly linked to the beat of the treadle that governs the speed of the wheel. (This effect is heightened by the fact that the reader always hears Schubert's setting in the inner ear.) Nerval attributes to Gretchen a flatter, more placid misery, as if she were drained of all hope, and Faust already dwelt in the past tense, a legendary figure like the king of Thule. But as we'll see, it was possible for French music to restore to Gretchen the heartbeat that the French verse lacked.

Soon after the translation appeared, the young Berlioz began work on a musical setting of some of the verse sections of Nerval's translations, *Huit scènes de Faust* (published in 1829), his Opus 1—but in 1829 or 1830 he withdrew the work and reassigned the opus number to his *Waverley* overture (published in 1839), for he understood that his embarkation on the Faust material was premature. Berlioz could not have been encouraged by Goethe's response to the *Huit scènes de Faust*: when Berlioz sent his score to the distinguised old poet, Goethe passed it on to his music adviser, Carl-Friedrich Zelter, who perceived only "sneezing, croaking, vomiting . . . a miscarriage from a hideous incest."[3] Posterity has not looked kindly on Zelter, who acted as a screen to insulate Goethe from some of the best settings of his poetry: but in a strange way Zelter was sensitive to the disturbing physiological intensity of Berlioz's work. Berlioz waited sixteen years, until 1845, before revisiting the material and deciding to commission a librettist, one Almire Gandonnière, to write some recitatives and other new text, so that Berlioz could create a much more substantial piece, *La damnation de Faust* (1846). But it is important to remember that the later composition is an expansion of a song cycle—not for a single voice, since it includes choral settings (such as the Easter hymn and the peasants' chorus), as well as settings of solo songs, notably for Marguerite and

Méphistophélès (in 1829, a tenor!)—but a song cycle nonetheless. *Roméo et Juliette* is a peculiar hybrid of opera and symphony; but *La damnation de Faust* is an elaborate and extensive set of vocal highlights, like excerpts from an unwritten opera, that grope for connection. As we've seen, Goethe constructed *Faust* piecemeal, by writing disjunct scenes and then writing interstitial matter; and Berlioz is exactly faithful to that compositional rhythm, in that he wrote music for the parts that cry out for music, and then pasted them together as best he could.

The new material added to the *Huit scènes de Faust* in 1845–46 consists of the most miscellaneous stuff imaginable: recitative and aria, march, fugue, minuet, pandemonium—a whole vaudeville farced into a pre-existent collection of songs and choruses. Like Goethe's poem, it seems to strive toward a condition of genrelessness; but some allusions to recognizable genres can be found. *La damnation de Faust* bears some relation to certain old, almost plotless operatic mélanges, desperately out of date by 1846, along the lines of such *opéra-ballets* as Rameau's *Les Indes galantes* (1735)—but Berlioz considered Rameau more a theorist than a composer, to judge from his published comments. Perhaps the closest formal analogue to *La damnation de Faust* among contemporary compositions is the Lisztian operatic fantasy, such as *Réminiscences de Don Juan* (1841), in which three striking themes from Mozart's *Don Giovanni* (1787) are presented, sometimes in fairly straightforward fashion, but often distended or accelerated, displaced, developed into strange episodes that provide connective tissue. *La damnation de Faust* is like a fantasy based on a non-existent opera, in which the singers and orchestra seem guided more by musical whim, by the need to astonish, spoof, devastate, than by the normal proprieties of operatic discourse.

Berlioz's *La damnation de Faust*

1. The Anti-Faust

The greater the character, the more exasperating the musical representation. For the artistic purposes of the last few centuries, the largest, the most resonant, the most mythically intriguing characters have been Don Juan and Faust; and yet, despite the best efforts of the ablest composers, the satyr and the scholar have both been strangely elusive, fugitive. Mozart's *Il dissoluto punito, ossia Il Don Giovanni* (1787) depicts energetically, subtly, brilliantly, the unstable ethical and erotic universe that Don Juan has built around himself; but Don Juan is underrepresented in that universe, with little to sing except a serenade, a seduction duet, some instructions to his servant, and a few vehement gestures of defiance. W. H. Auden (following Kierkegaard) has described Mozart's Don Juan as an emptiness, a creature totally lacking in purpose or goal, a zero man who seduces an infinite series of women only because this arbitrary, absurd goal serves to conceal his sheer aimlessness of being—his "pleasure in seducing women is not sensual but arithmetical."[1] Similarly, Paul Griffiths has described Mozart's Don Juan as a kind of amnesic, living in the shallows of the immediate present, a vacant center in the opera in which he stars.[2] According to twentieth-century critics, then, Mozart faced the perplexity of describing a character who is more voracious than a man but less than human.

When we turn from the romancer to the necromancer, we discover that Faust, as a musical hero, has similar metaphysical defects. Composers revel in Gretchen, in Mephistopheles, in the panoply of weird apparitions, but Faust himself presents difficulties. Berlioz was the first significant composer to attempt a large-scale musical response to Goethe's *Faust*; and Berlioz's every instinct led him to ignore the main character in favor of the peripheries—to eviscerate Goethe's Faust, to evacuate him. Indeed, in the *Huit scènes de Faust,* Faust does not appear at all. This odd feature derives from Nerval's decision to split Goethe's poem into prose and poetry: Nerval (perhaps without intending to do so) demotes Faust into an overwhelmingly prosaic character, so incapable of carrying a tune that he needs Méphistophélès to do his serenading for him (l. 3682). In the old semi-operas of England, the hero (King Arthur, Prospero, Diocletian) never sang—

the singing scenes were given to specialists, not to the stars of the stage; and Nerval's text exactly reflects this model, by placing a talky protagonist in the midst of vivid, volatile characters always ready to break out in song. It is not surprising, then, that when Faust does appear in Berlioz's music, in *La damnation de Faust,* he turns out to be a tentative, desultory, fretful thing, peculiarly unresponsive to the world he beholds—again, a kind of zero man.

La damnation de Faust is a point of convergence where a juiced-up song cycle meets a condensed opera, an opera with all blubber cut away. Berlioz's comments on Mozart show how the procedure worked: in his *Mémoires* Berlioz wrote that *Don Giovanni* was all the rage during his youth, and that he would shed his heart's blood if he could erase the "indecent clowning" of the cabaletta to Donna Anna's *Non mi dir*—a "song of profound sadness, in which all the poetry of love is wept out in tears of grief, and in which one nevertheless finds toward the end of the piece some ridiculous and shockingly inappropriate notes."[3] *La damnation de Faust* is a kind of *Don Giovanni* deconventionalized, with all the repellent operatic elements removed; in both works a figment of extreme desire crashes against the limits of the space in which human desire can operate. But Berlioz's hero is far weaker, far more bored and petulant than Mozart's Don Juan or Goethe's Faust; and here I'll examine Berlioz's modes of nullity, and speculate on Berlioz's reasons for offering such a shrunken image of Faust.

Some of the responsibility for Faust's diminishment lies not with Berlioz but with Goethe himself, who took the vehement magus of the chapbook and the puppet plays and made him an intellectual, a theoretician of desire. As Katherine Reeve points out, when Madame de Staël read Goethe's *Faust,* she was repelled by the hero's lassitude and passivity, and considered Mephistopheles the hero of the poem;[4] but Goethe's Faust at his limpest is a tower of strength compared to Berlioz's sputtery, languid Faust. One recent critic, Hermann Hofer, has even argued, with great erudition and cogency, that Berlioz deliberately, daringly, farsightedly, created Faust as a vain aesthete, a tourist even when at home, sexually impotent, incapable of political action or of sympathy for his fellow man, in order to illustrate the collapse of certain illusions about the possibilities of human progress—an example of disenchantment with Romanticism occurring within the domain of Romanticism itself. For Hofer, Berlioz's Faust is not so much above human action as beneath it. Hofer—remembering that Goethe's Faust announced grandly, "In the beginning was the Deed" (l. 1237)—even describes Berlioz's Faust as a kind of revocation of Goethe's, a terminus: "Faust hat endgültig Abschied genommen von seinem Tat-Mythos" ("Faust has finally taken leave from his Myth of the Deed").[5] Not all scholars of Berlioz agree with this line of argument—Reeve, for example, provides a subtly qualified, highly intelligent defense of the right of Berlioz's Faust to the salvation that Berlioz denied him. I'm sympathetic to Hofer's claim that

Berlioz's Faust is infatuated with the void, trapped in hell, in a sense, even before any devil appears. But, of course, this self-annihilating quality of Faust is far from unique to Berlioz's work, and does not need to be explained (as Hofer explains it) as a reaction to the revolutionary movements in the European politics of the 1830s and 1840s; all Fausts are parodists, renouncers, revokers, from the Faust of the original 1587 chapbook, whose final meeting with his students is a morbid spoof of Christ's Last Supper, to the hero of Thomas Mann's *Doktor Faustus* (1947), who attempts to undo the finale of Beethoven's Ninth Symphony.[6] It is the duty of each Faust, in a sense, to dwell in a state of general contradiction—and even to constitute himself in contradiction to previous versions of Faust. Berlioz's Faust seems to me neither the end of a myth, nor even a deviation from a certain line of mythic development; instead, he seems merely to make unusually explicit the bizarre nonentity of all Fausts.

2. Berlioz contra Goethe

Goethe's *Faust* is a parable about wishing; near the beginning, in the Prologue in Heaven, God and Mephistopheles contrive a psychological experiment in which Faust is to be guinea pig: what will become of a man whose every desire is gratified? This experiment is, of course, exactly opposite to that in the book of Job, where God and Satan speculate on what will become of a man whose every desire is thwarted; but Faust is so trapped in a hollow world of illusory fulfillments that (at the end of Part One) he cries out Job's cry, O would I had never been born. Goethe so arranges his poem that the object of desire is displaced onto increasingly fantastical entities, until Faust is unable to discriminate between mere phantoms, like the specular image of the woman whom he sees in the witch's kitchen scene (l. 2600), and such vulnerable, pitiable objects as Gretchen. Goethe's *Faust,* then, can be considered as an exploration of unreality designed to teach the hero about the limits of the real, about the proper scope for human action.

But Berlioz's version means differently. It is not a story about a violent man who invokes a genie that can grant wishes; it is a story about a passive, strangely neutral man, so apathetic that he needs artificial stimulation if he is to feel anything at all. In Goethe's poem, there is continual displacement of the desired object; but in Berlioz's work, the desire itself is displaced, surgically removed from Faust and inserted into the breast of a companionable demon. Berlioz's Faust would like to join the peasants in their frolic, but cannot, indeed he envies the peasants their capacity for feeling—*De leurs plaisirs ma misère est jalouse*; then he looks at Hungarian soldiers marching off to war, and envies them their capacity for feeling—*Tout coeur frémit à leur chant de victoire; Le mien seul reste froid, insensible à la gloire* (All hearts thrill to their victory song; Mine alone stays cold, numb to all glory). He is a dead frog seeking Prof. Galvani for an electric charge. To some extent the Easter chorus can revive his extinct sensibility; but it is finally Méphistophélès who provides the goad that drives him. Berlioz wrote into Méphistophélès' music many opportunities for smirking, for laughter, for irony, even for sexual display, whereas Faust's music, in the opening scenes, suggests a sparse, flattened emotional land-scape; it is as if all the emotional volatility of Goethe's Faust has been transferred to the devil, leaving Berlioz's Faust desolate and cold, contem-plating suicide less for the sake of relieving despair than for the sake of evoking some sort of feeling in his unfeeling soul.

Goethe, of course, imagined Faust as a man who feels intensely and wishes to feel still more intensely—who hopes to experience "the whole tumult, the most painful joy, the dear hate, the quickening discontent" (ll. 1766–67). But, soon after Faust announces this program, Mephistopheles replies:

> You are in the end—just what you are.
> You can put on a wig with millions of locks,
> you can put your feet in elevator socks,—
> you always remain, just what you are. (ll. 1806–9)

Berlioz never set any of this scene to music, but these lines perhaps hold the key to Berlioz's construction of Faust's character. Berlioz beheld Faust from Mephistopheles' point of view, as a kind of inflatable doll, dressed up in all sorts of big costumes, but small, empty at the core. Faust is the lead tenor, but Méphistophélès is the impresario, investing Faust with tunes, costumes, and stage settings for his performance. This is not Goethe's version of Faust, precisely, but it is an interpretation latent in Goethe's text—Berlioz, with his tremendous deconstructive power, simply actualizes a Faust that lies half-buried in Goethe's poem.

Berlioz's Faust belongs to a well-defined genus of hero, a genus derived from Byron. It might be argued that Goethe's Faust is one of the ancestors of the Byronic hero, since Byron wrote *Manfred* (1817) in a fit of inspira-tion after hearing an impromptu translation of a few passages of Goethe's *Faust,* a poem which Byron had not read. (And insofar as the Euphorion of Goethe's *Faust* is based on Byron, the Byronic hero was to become in-volved in the very poem that helped to inspire him.) But the Byronic hero exaggerates the estrangement, the disaffection, the omnivorousness of the Faustian hero, to a degree beyond anything in Goethe. Because the Byronic hero belongs nowhere, he identifies himself with everything—his ego-sys-tem is monstrously distended, engorged:

> I live not in myself, but I become
> Portion of that around me; and to me,

> High mountains are a feeling, but the hum
> Of human cities torture: I can see
> Nothing to loathe in nature, save to be
> A link reluctant in a fleshly chain,
> Class'd among creatures, when the soul can flee,
> And with the sky, the peak, the heaving plain
> Of ocean, or the stars, mingle, and not in vain.
>   (*Childe Harold's Pilgrimage* 3.72)[7]

Berlioz, of course, knew this poem well, and used it for the program of his symphony with viola obbligato *Harold en Italie* (1834). In his *Mémoires* Berlioz wrote a fascinating commentary:

> I thought of writing an orchestral suite of scenes, into which the solo viola would find itself (in varying degrees) mixed, like an actual person, always staying in character; by placing the viola in the midst of the poetic memories I retained from my wanderings in the Abruzzi, I wanted to make it a sort of melancholy dreamer like Byron's Childe Harold. . . . As in the *Symphonie fantastique,* one principal theme (the first tune of the viola) is reproduced throughout the work; but with this difference, that the theme of the *Symphonie fantastique,* the *idée fixe,* interposes itself obstinately, as a fleeting idea of passion, a diversion, into scenes where it doesn't belong, while Harold's tune superimposes itself onto the other orchestral tunes, with which it contrasts in movement and in character, without interrupting their development.[8]

Berlioz's Harold, like Byron's, is simultaneously conspicuous and unobtrusive: he belongs nowhere and everywhere, inhabits his own static plane of discourse that modifies nothing around it, borrows nothing from it. I believe that, when Berlioz revised the *Huit scènes de Faust* into *La damnation de Faust,* he invented a Faust character along lines similar to Harold: an abstract, unbothersome presence who could be fitted into the whole work anywhere, without interrupting the development. Indeed Faust is even less obtrusive than Harold, in that Faust does not even have a persistent musical theme to call his own;[9] indeed there are moments when Faust simply glides over and around any musical material that happens to be handy. Sometimes Berlioz merely composed an independent, not very dissonant tenor line for Faust over pre-existing music, as in the Easter chorus. Sometimes Berlioz used Faust-recitatives as connective tissue between scenes. Sometimes Berlioz composed special numbers for Faust, of an unusual character; but before I discuss the newly composed Faust music of 1846, I must discuss the sort of music that Berlioz thought appropriate for Romantic heroes and heroines.

3. Psychological Melodies

As many critics have noted, there is a special sort of melody—far from typical of Berlioz's usual melodic practice—that Berlioz reserves for certain important musical events: long, monolinear, inconclusive, vague, at once restless and immobile, infinitely susceptible to variation but with such low original profile that no variant will seem especially deviant or significant. Such is the nature of the *idée fixe* of the *Symphonie fantastique* (1830); such is the nature of the *Andante malinconico e sostenuto* in the *Roméo seul* movement of *Roméo et Juliette* (1839). These themes tend to be strongly *espressivo*, but it is hard to specify exactly what emotion they express— they aren't legible according to the normal musical codes for denoting tenderness, or anger, or despair, or even (I think) the melancholy implied by the direction *Andante malincolico*. These themes are so long and vagrant that they scarcely seem to pertain to a single state of feeling. If there is such a thing as generic expression, expression expressive of nothing in particular, these themes come close to it. Such themes are useful for Romantic protagonists, who refuse any definition of identity, who will not be confined to a particular shape; the theme itself becomes Proteus, capable of myriad inflections but so inherently shapeless that all inflection tends to disappear into its general diffuseness of being. Berlioz had an amazing ability to invent potent but recessive, difficult-to-remember themes. These themes have little or nothing in common with the striking tunes that Liszt invented to illustrate his thesis that any emotional content could be squeezed out of any series of pitches; with Liszt and Wagner the listener usually feels that there exists a single prime form of the theme from which any variation is measurably deviant; but what is the prime form of Berlioz's *idée fixe*? Phrases from it appear easily in the memory, a swaying, a feeling of melodic vagrancy; but the whole tends to dance away from the mind that tries to grasp it.

I know of nothing in music before Berlioz's time in which the composer invents a melody for the sake of being difficult to comprehend; in which the composer, by means of the ear's struggle to apprehend a melody, tries to imitate the mind's struggle to think. There are certainly many cases of playfully concealed tunes in earlier music, perhaps starting with the parody masses of the middle ages; certainly in the Quodlibet in Bach's Goldberg variations; and in the twenty-second Diabelli variation Beethoven plays an astonishing perceptual game, so equivocating between Diabelli's waltz and Mozart's *Notte e giorno faticar* that the tune becomes comparable to that Gestalt-psychological diagram that can be apprehended either as a rabbit or as a duck. But these composers do not use *trompe-l'oreille* for the purpose of representing a person; that is Berlioz's discovery, that certain difficult melodies could represent the involutions of subjectivity—not a par-

Example 14. *Symphonie fantastique,* theme of the Introduction

ticular feeling, not sadness or fear or triumph, but the general process of apperception in the human mind. One might refer to these melodies as psychological melodies.

The evolution of the *idée fixe* shows that it was never a melody that denoted a specific state of mind, but always a melody that denoted the whole process of mentality itself. The first public (or semi-public) appearance of the *idée fixe* came at the beginning of the Prix de Rome cantata *Herminie* (1828). If pressed to describe the character of this tune, I might describe it as jumpy, nervous, unsettled. The pagan Herminie is in love with the Christian hero Tancrède, who has ravaged her Syrian homeland; yet she cherishes the weight of the chains that bind her to her love. Her emotions are complex—love, hate, anger, grief, shame, terror, all commingled; and in this way the tune is turning into a psychological melody, suggestive of a general arousal of sensibility, not a finite feeling. Later in the cantata it reappears to accompany the words *J'exhale en vain ma plainte fugitive, Je l'implore, il ne m'entend pas* (In vain I breathe out my fleeting lament, I implore him, he hears me not)—as if the tune represented an emotion incapable of expression, too deep for words or song, an audible inaudibility. And the tune appears still later when Herminie wonders whether she might herself wield a lance to help save Tancrède—or is she too weak? *Tancrède va mourir peut-être, et je balance!* (Tancrède may die, and I waver!). Again the tune suggests irresolute, indeterminate, equivocal states of mind, an extremely tense hesitation. The tune is now ready for the full metaphysical promotion it receives the very next year, when it becomes the *idée fixe*—the motto, first heard as the first theme of the exposition in the *Symphonie fantastique.*

The introduction to the symphony is, like the *idée fixe,* a psychlogical sort of melody, and based on pre-existing material. Berlioz noted in his *Mémoires* that the introduction tune (example 14) first appeared in a juvenile song-setting, later destroyed, of the "pale poesy" of Florian's *Estelle*—an "extremely sad" song about leaving home and mistress forever.[10] But in the program to the symphony, Berlioz describes the mood of the tune, not as "extremely sad," but as emotionally diffuse, pertinent to *le vague des passions* (example 15). The two melodies are not identical, but they are congruent.[11] They share two features: first, the salient figure of an up-and-down slip of a semitone drooping into a descending scale; and second, an

Example 15. *Symphonie fantastique, idée fixe*

extraordinary vagueness. According to the program, the *idée fixe* is a tune with the same characteristics as the ideal woman herself, *passionné, mais noble et timide*—again, as in *Herminie,* the tune seems unable to make up its mind whether it is going to express itself or to refrain from expression, to declare its intensities out loud or to grow shy and reticent.

Some of the best musicians of Berlioz's time were perplexed about the nature of the *idée fixe*; if the melody was intended to represent an obsession, a mental disease, that disease turned out to be contagious. For example, Liszt wrote a strangely irresolute nocturne (1846) recasting the tune (*L'idée fixe / Andante amoroso d'après une mélodie de Berlioz*—S. 395); and Schumann's important essay (1835) on the *Symphonie fantastique* suggests his profound difficulty in trying to construe the emotional and musical attributes of the tune. In one passage Schumann (as Florestan) wrote, "There he sees her! I picture this feminine creature as I picture the main theme of the whole symphony,—pale, slender as a lily, veiled, still, almost cold;—but the word grows sleepy and its tones burn into the vitals."[12] But later, Schumann, now speaking as himself, not Florestan, considered the tune more skeptically:

> True, the principal melody of the symphony is a bit common. . . . But then one should remember that it was not his intention to represent a great thought, but rather a persistent, torturing idea, the kind of thing one carries around for days without being able to get it out of one's head; and this suggestion of something monotonous, maddening, could hardly have been more successfully accomplished.[13]

No critic has been more sensitive than Schumann to the E. T. A. Hoffmann-like (or Poe-like) qualities of the *Symphonie fantastique*; and yet, Schumann's description of the *idée fixe* is a mass of contradictions: cold but burning; veiled but monotonous; common but maddening. This sense that the *idée fixe* is oxymoronic, incapable of definition, can also be found in Schumann's description of its resistance to harmony: Berlioz's "melodies are distinguished by such an intensity of each individual note that, like many old folk tunes, they simply cannot accommodate any harmonic accompaniment, and would often be the poorer, tonally, for being assigned one."[14] The *idée fixe,* then, fascinates in the manner of a Rorschach ink blot: it has no shape or character, but a thousand shapes or characters can be projected into it.

Perhaps the most startling of all of Schumann's comments is his bizarre comparision of the *Symphonie fantastique* to upside-down music: "As as child I used to place the music upside down on the music stand and revel in the strangely intertwined notational structures—as I subsequently revelled in the upside-down palaces reflected in the canals of Venice."[15] Berlioz's work does indeed manifest odd and dislocating perspectives—like Sara in *Sara la baigneuse* (1834), where Sara's image in the water is musically symbolized by mirror-like passages in contrary motion, Berlioz may have liked to stare at his own water-reflection, for the *Symphonie fantastique* offers an unsettled, shimmery, broken image of the composer himself and of the whole genre of the symphony. The great novelty of Berlioz's first symphony is the discrimination of two musical planes, the plane of the ordinary musical discourse—the symphony as it would be understood by Haydn—and the psychological plane, inhabited by the *idée fixe,* where we hear the composer in the act of inventing his symphony, toying with ideas, commenting on the music, criticizing his composition as he writes it. Berlioz was one of the finest music critics of his generation, and the *Symphonie fantastique* contrives a method for including a critical intelligence, detached, sometimes (in the later movements) completely disengaged from the symphonic argument, thinking about something else entirely, in the text of the symphony itself. Berlioz understood that if music is to grow fully self-conscious, in the approved nineteenth-century manner, it had to divide into two levels of discourse. All self-consciousness posits two selves, a self that looks and a self that is looked at; a nominative self and an accusative self; an *I* and a *me.* The *Symphonie fantastique* replaces the ordinary symphonic tension between the two thematic groups of the exposition with the tension between the giddy, plastic, speculative self and the settled, historical accusative self. Schoenberg thought that Bach enjoyed making the ricercars in his *Musikalisches Opfer* out of the king's theme precisely because the theme was so extremely resistant to fugal treatment;[16] similarly, it is possible that Berlioz chose the *idée fixe* for the first theme of a symphonic allegro precisely because it was so unsymphonizable, so obstinately unsusceptible to development with other themes. It can be argued that Berlioz did achieve a symphonic allegro; but in another sense the *Symphonie fantastique* is an anti-symphony, a musical depiction of the process of thematic detachment, not of thematic combination. The *idée fixe* persists in inhabiting its own space; it is an atmosphere, a lens, not an obedient, compliant, composable entity. Berlioz uses the *idée fixe* to dramatize the mind's struggle to watch, to assimilate, to criticize the experience of the body. The whole structure of the *Symphonie fantastique* is a Byronic structure of self-consciousness, self-estrangement.

Because opium supposedly tends to enforce a separation between these two selves, it was convenient for Berlioz to make his symphonist an opium eater, dreamily detached from his usual identity. On the lower, representational plane of the symphony, the personage dances at a ball, or strolls in the countryside as the weather turns threatening; on the upper plane of the symphony, he watches himself, becomes fascinated with himself, or simply ignores himself and concentrates on his private delirium, the *idée fixe.* Beethoven noted that his Sixth Symphony was less painting than an expression of feelings; but Berlioz wished first to paint, then to show how overwhelming feelings lead to a distortion of the painting: the objective music, such as the orchestra at the ball or the shepherds' piping, is increasingly deformed, twisted by the plastic stress of emotion into false expressivity—false, because the loneliness represented by the unanswered piping (at the end of the third movement) pertains less to the shepherd who pipes than to the composer's listening mind, searching through nature for mood-symbols for its own states. By the last two movements, there are still remembered remnants of "objective" music—a death-march, a round dance, the *Dies irae*—but by now the lower plane, the plane of the scrutinized, is itself as hallucinatory and unstable as the upper plane, where the watcher watches. The horror of the March to the Scaffold is, as the program makes explicit, the horror of beholding one's own death—the ultimate exercise of Romantic self-consciousness. This jagged, abrupt intrusion of self-consciousness into music (as shown by the inserted musically irrelevant quotation of the *idée fixe*) is oddly anticipated by the finale of the other most ambitious symphony of the time, Beethoven's Ninth (1824), in which a critical intelligence—the composer's own self-exasperation, it seems—suddenly interrupts the concert by shouting, *O Freunde, nicht diese Töne*: anything but *this* noise, my friends.

When we come to the final movement of the *Symphonie fantastique,* the Sabbath Round, we are in the world of Goethe's *Faust*. It is possible that the movement was originally written for a projected Faust ballet; in any case, Berlioz affirmed that the whole symphony was written under the influence of Goethe's poem, and the movement clearly alludes to Goethe's Walpurgisnight—the obsessive woman is now a version of mutilated Gretchen, joining the revels for the sake of provoking the hero to despair. There are indeed a number of structural parallels between the *Symphonie fantastique* and *La damnation de Faust*: for example, Faust lifts to his lips a vial of poison—an even stronger poison than opium—but Méphistophélès appears instead, a kind of poison-surrogate, to induce Faust to dreams every bit as hallucinatory as the opium-dreams of the symphony. Furthermore, Faust's character is constructed as psychological, nominative, according to the recipe of the symphony; but with this difference, that Faust is a spectator who lacks a self to look at, a blank *I* without a *me*. Who is

Faust? Berlioz makes nothing of the celebrated scene found in the chap-book, in Marlowe, in all the puppet plays, in Goethe, later in Gounod, where the disgusted Faust casts away his books and expostulates on the futility of scholarship. Berlioz's Faust has no history, no prior personal relationships, no laboratory assistant; he seems to have been newly created on the day when the action begins. He is a figment of estrangement and derangement, without character, without predicate.

4. Feigned Opera

During the first bars of *La damnation de Faust,* we hear an unaccompa-nied melody; then Faust immediately begins a paean to spring, *Le vieil hiver* (example 16). What does the music mean? Like language, music ac-quires its meaning through the intersection of contexts; but, as is not the case with language, the rules by which music acquires meaning also shift with the context. The first context of the opening tune of *La damnation de Faust* is the class of psychological melodies, such as the *idée fixe* and Roméo's lonely theme: it is long, slow, monolinear, self-overlapping, with no strongly determinate shape or certain harmonic structure. But there is another con-text for *Le vieil hiver* as well, audible in the rising scale around which it is constructed. In Romantic music throughout Europe, melodies with simple, prominent scales, rising through at least six degrees, are typically felt ap-propriate for spring songs: *Der Frühling will kommen* (Spring will come), sings the soprano in Schubert's *Der Hirt auf dem Felsen* (1828), to a care-free, effortless ascending scale; in the introduction to Glinka's *A Life for the Tsar* (1836), the chorus sings *Vesna svoe vzjala* (Spring has arrived) to the same sort of figure; Mendelssohn's *Der Blumenstrauss* (The Bouquet, 1832) opens with a strain that moves lightly up the scale—"she wanders in the flower garden and gazes at the riot of blossom"; somewhat later, Gounod's song *Au printemps* (To Spring, 1868) begins in this manner, too.[17] Obviously, a large chunk of scale would not be out of place in a tonal song, no matter what its subject matter; but spring songs seem especially ame-nable to artless, uninflected melodies—and the scale is the least artificial, the least elaborate, of melodies. Berlioz himself wrote a spring song with a prominent rising scale, the *Villanelle* in *Les nuits d'été* (1841—example 17), which shares with *Le vieil hiver* a dotted rhythm as well. Therefore the opening melody of *La damnation de Faust* can be heard as a kind of na-ture-theme, though far less resolute, less contoured, less rhythmically heady than that of the *Villanelle*. Like Wagner (*Eine Faust-Ouvertüre,* 1840) and Liszt (*Eine Faust-Symphonie,* 1857), Berlioz begins his Faust-composition with a musical question mark, a question without an answer. We begin, then, with an aria that seems to mean nature, but nature bleached, en-

Andante placido, non troppo lento (♪ = 152)

Example 16. Faust's paean to spring

Allegretto (♩ = 96)

Quand vien- dra   la sai-son nou - vel - le,   Quand au-ront dis-pa - ru les froids,

Example 17. *Les nuits d'été: Villanelle*

feebled, overplacid, made moody and subjective; there is the sense of a
mind brooding on natural delights but unable fully to participate in them.
As the aria continues, Berlioz decorates the melody with bird-songs and
other beauties, but it keeps refining itself back down to the single line, as if
Faust's mental alienation must keep reasserting itself; the melody shakes
itself free from harmony and ornament, all that is extrinsic to it naked
purity. When the peasants come with their sexy chorus, Faust can only
interrupt it with his own white, immiscible tune, incapable of blending
with other voices. When the soldiers come, Faust can only vanish and listen—his own musical speech is too fragile to assert itself in the midst of
such a tremendous outpouring of energy. Berlioz endured much criticism
for transposing his first scene to Hungary, purely for the sake of introducing the Rákóczy March; Berlioz replied, quite reasonably, that "the most
eccentric voyages may be attributed to a personage like Faust, without
offending probability in any way."[18] One might even guess that Berlioz
wanted his auditors to enter a musically as well as a geographically random world, in which any musical form or mode might suddenly pop up.
La damnation de Faust goes still further than *Roméo et Juliette* in the direction of sheer genrelessness; Faust's mind is a blank screen, a tabula rasa,
on which any picture, any sort of musical composition, may take shape,
without regard to the formal propriety of opera or symphony or any known
genre.

La damnation de Faust may be miscellaneous in character, structurally
challenging, but each of the four parts is governed by a tendency to build
to a noisy climax—the dramatic rhythm of the circus or magic show or the
virtuoso star-turn opera, where each impressive number must be capped
by some still more stupendous tour de force:

Partie Scène
I   1   *Plaines de Hongrie* (Plains of Hungary)
    2   *Ronde des paysans* (Peasants' round dance)
    3   *Une autre partie de la plaine* (Another part of the plain)
               Marche hongroise (Hungarian march)
II 4   *Nord de l'Allemagne* (Northern Germany)
               Chant de la Fête de Pâques (Easter hymn)
    5
    6   *La cave d'Auerbach à Leipzig* (Auerbach's cellar in
               Leipzig)
               Choeur de buveurs (Drinking chorus)
               Chanson de Brander (Brander's song)
               Fugue sur le thème de la chanson de Brander (Fugue on
               the theme of Brander's song)
               Chanson de Méphistophélès (Mephistopheles' song)
    7   *Bosquets et Prairies au Bord de l'Elbe—Air de
               Méphistophélès* (Woods and meadows on the banks of
               the Elbe—Mephistopheles' aria)
               Choeur de gnomes et de sylphes—Songe de Faust
               (Chorus of gnomes and sylphs—Faust's dream)
               Ballet des sylphes (Ballet of the sylphs)
    8   *Final—Choeur d'étudiants et de soldats* (Finale—Chorus
               of students and soldiers
III 9   *Tambours et trompettes sonnant la retraite* (Drums and
               trumpets sounding the retreat)
               Air de Faust (Faust's aria)
    10
    11   *Le roi de Thulé, chanson gothique* (The King of Thule,
               gothic song)
    12   *Evocation*
               Menuet des follets (Minuet of the will-o'-the-wisps)
               Sérénade de Méphistophélès (Mephistopheles' serenade)
    13   *Final: Duo* (Finale: Duet)
    14   *Trio et Choeur* (Trio and chorus)
IV 15   *Romance*
    16   *Invocation à la nature* (Invocation to nature)
    17   *Récitatif et chasse* (Recitative and hunt)
    18   *La course à l'abîme* (The ride to the abyss)
    19   *Pandaemonium*
    Epilogue   *Sur la terre* (On earth)
               Dans le ciel (In heaven)
               Apothéose de Marguerite (Marguerite's Apotheosis)
(The untitled entries in this outline[19] represent brief passages, usually of
recitative.)

Part I ends with an army's brilliant march, Part II with rowdy students and soldiers, Part III with a hue and cry of scandalized neighbors, and Part IV with the most ghastly ruckus in all mid-nineteenth-century music—before the celestial languors of the Epilogue propose an alternative of bliss. The soldiers and the students of the first two parts simply shoulder the introverted scholar aside as they go about their loud business—they leave him little room to maneuver, to assert himself, to utter his pale soliloquies. But the townspeople of the third part hunt him down, as if they want to silence the little tenor; and, of course, the demons of the fourth part finally unman him, unFaust him, out once and for all. Faust tries to step into the spotlight, to interrupt the strident medley of marches, drinking songs, dramatic ballads, superior hoochie-koochie dances, and to claim priority—This is *my* stage! But the more aggressively he struggles to make himself heard, the more strongly the other performers, singly or in chorus, beat him down.

   This is not to say that Faust is utterly incapable of assuming a public character, interacting with the rest of the cast. In the third part of the Dramatic Legend—as Berlioz called *La damnation de Faust,* since he had to call it something—we see a Faust quite different from that of the first part. Under the influence of Méphistophélès, Faust decides to experiment with a role, a self, that of the lead tenor in an opera; he descends from the plane of speculation to the plane of action. He sings a suitably operatic (that is, histrionically intimate) aria, *Merci, doux crépuscule,* in which he admires the atmosphere of Marguerite's room—perhaps only the chromatic phrase after *Que j'aime à contempler ton chevet virginal* (How I love to watch your virginal bedstead) betrays the sinisterness, the unreality, of Faust's posture as mellifluous lover. And Faust and Marguerite sing a suitably tasteful duet, *Ange adoré,* but this duet presently degenerates into a trio with chorus as Méphistophélès interrupts the lovers' frail glee. It is instructive to compare this duet and trio with the *Roméo seul* movement of *Roméo et Juliette,* in which a *larghetto espressivo* theme, representative of Roméo's musing on love, is first interrupted by, then combined with, an *allegro* theme representative of the ball at the Capulets'. In both works, the music of private intensities has to compete against the music of public event; but Roméo manages loudly, triumphantly, to sustain his private vision in counterpoint with the festive dance, whereas Faust and Marguerite are simply drowned out by the urgencies of Méphistophélès, the obscene mockery of the chorus. Roméo makes himself heard; but the little voice of Faust is easily overwhelmed. Indeed it might even be argued that musically—not verbally—Faust and Marguerite end by joining the chorus and mocking themselves: the material sung by the lovers, during the final part of the trio, also tends to be disruptive, strident, in the same manner as that of the chorus. Faust is by nature so much a spectator, not an actor, that he cannot help abstracting himself, even in the midst of a love duet.

The trio perfectly illustrates the centrifugal quality of Berlioz's imagination throughout *La damnation de Faust*: he piles unrelated planes of musical discourse on top of one another, partly as an abstract game to show off his contrapuntal ingenuity, partly as a serious inquiry into the fragmentation of Faust's universe in the absence of an effective, stable, coordinating sensibility at its core. The lamination of Faust's various domains of desire grows hopelessly frayed, in the presence of such a querulous inept Faust; and so Berlioz continually superimposes incommensurable events, to hint at a pandemonium that lurks in every corner of his dramatic legend, not simply the final scene. Faust, in Part One of Goethe's poem, was more or less able to subordinate his whole environment to his restless, brooding fantasy; but Berlioz's slacker Faust doesn't have enough energy to unify the disparate materials of his life—and so Berlioz creates A B A/B structures, less as a private alternative of sonata form (as in *Roméo et Juliette*) than as a way of indicating the glistening absence of relation between A and B. At the end of the second part there is a chorus of soldiers, followed by a chorus of students, followed by "Les deux choeurs réunis"—one on top of the other. At the end of the third part there is the squash of love duet, Méphistophélès, and chorus of derision, an *English concert* of various groups of frantic deaf people singing at the same time. And near the end of the fourth part comes the official pandemonium, to which all these little pandemonia have been pointing. When the imagination loses hold on its images, they grow into autonomous, clashing things. In Wölfflin's terms, *La damnation de Faust* is Southern art, a caricature of Southern art: the depicted phenomena become so distinct, so isolated, that they seem to inhabit different planes of being. Instead of an opera, *La damnation de Faust* is a flattened, unconsecutive sort of drama, a three-ring circus, in which the tender love duet and the furious chorus of townspeople are co-present, oblivious of one another; swivel your neck and you can see the sword-swallower, or the lion-tamer, or the bareback rider, for all the acts are going on at the same time.

The purpose—or studied purposelessness—of these musical incongruities is suggested by one of Berlioz's most fascinating comments on his music, his account of a Dresden performance of *La damnation de Faust*. Berlioz recalls the *Amen* fugue for a chorus of drunkards that he added in 1846 to his old setting of Brander's *chanson*:

> The chorus takes up, in a large-scale movement, the *theme of the song of the rat,* and makes a genuine scholastico-classical fugue, in which the chorus sometimes vocalizes on *a a a a,* sometimes rapidly repeats the whole word, *amen, amen, amen,* accompanied by tuba, ophicleide, bassoon, and double basses. This fugue is written according to the most severe rules of counterpoint, and, in spite of the insensate brutality of its style, and the impious and blasphemous contrast intentionally estab-

lished between the musical expression and the meaning of the word
amen . . . the public is not at all shocked, and the harmonious ensemble
that results from the weave of notes in this scene is always and everywhere applauded. . . .

A music lover came up to me during an intermission. . . . he ap-
proached me with a timid smile:

—Your fugue on *amen* is ironical, isn't it?

—Alas, sir, I'm afraid so!

He wasn't certain!!![20]

La damnation de Faust is one continuous irony, full of false agreement
between style and substance, full of self-conscious inauthenticities of musical discourse. Indeed the work is *about* falseness, about the parodies of
genius that come to pass when a small man wraps himself in magic robes
too big for him. In some sense Berlioz seems to conceive Faust according to
a model derived from another poem of Goethe's, *Der Zauberlehrling,* the
sorcerer's apprentice.

Part Four begins with two arias, one for Marguerite and one for Faust:
their contrast is instructive, for Marguerite establishes a powerful subjectivity, grows potent, whereas Faust diminishes. This is an important rhythm
in Berlioz's drama, for as Faust abdicates all authority of imagination, the
other characters develop heft and personality, tensile strength.

Marguerite's aria is the spinning song, Nerval's equivalent (with some
modifications by Berlioz) to *Meine Ruh ist hin.* Schubert's Gretchen suffers
continually from severe *Angst,* a bad case of nerves; but Berlioz's manifests
a remarkable range of feeling. At the beginning, Berlioz spins out a long-
breathed cantilena, first for cor anglais, then for voice, almost in contradiction to the fairly short lines of the poem: Gretchen seems to be in a state of
drowsy reverie, musing over her dreams of Faust. But soon the aria starts
to grow more rhythmically intent: in the stanza where Marguerite men-
tions her fainting heartbeat—*Mon faible coeur s'arrête, Puis se glace
aussitôt*—the accompaniment develops into a murmur of staccato eighth-
note chords, with an *fp* thud at the beginning of each bar, ominously halt-
ing on a fermata rest, as if her heart were skipping a beat (example 18).
Later, Marguerite gets excited at the thought of seeing Faust at her window—*Mon coeur bat, mon coeur bat et se presse*—and the accompaniment goes into a flurry of little paired figures, sharply accented, a case of
complete orchestral tachycardia (example 19). Berlioz's Marguerite—like
Schubert's—dwells in a vivid present tense: she doesn't simply remember,
she *relives* the history of her love, in all its elation and wretchedness. The
theme of love here, as elsewhere, stimulated Berlioz's musical imagination
to a full seizure of human biorhythms.

Marguerite's aria concerns her intense possession of her experience;
Faust's aria, by contrast, concerns his inadequacy to his experience. In his

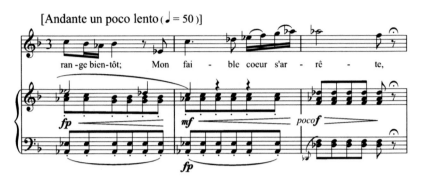

Example 18. Marguerite's heart-skip

Example 19. Marguerite's tachycardia

Example 20. Nature's bass

aria, *Nature immense* (example 20), he loses his operatic role, reverts explicitly to the helpless onlooker of the first part. *Nature immense* is, like Faust's opening aria *Le vieil hiver,* preoccupied with the intellectual's relation to the earth, but it is a different kind of aria completely: here the orchestra plays an *andante maestoso* expressing the power and majesty of nature—the deep bass consists of rising and falling scales, in dotted rhythms, somewhat like those that Wagner later used, in *Der Ring des Nibelungen,* to symbolize Erda, the world's understructure, the stamina of things. As we've seen, dotted scalar figures appeared in *Le vieil hiver,* an indeterminate musing about the approach of spring; but now such nature figures have detached themselves from Faust's voice, and have gained such power that they seem in danger of crushing him.[21] Faust still wishes to join his song to nature's—*À vos bruits souverains ma voix aime à s'unir.* At most he occasionally can follow the grand bass line, as at the phrase *soufflez, ouragans* or *croulez, rochers*; sometimes he manages to sing other snatches of melody; but the accompaniment is far more impressive than what Faust sings. Grétry complained that Gluck had put the pedestal on stage and stuck the statue in the orchestra;[22] but I imagine that no aria of Gluck's would seem (if deprived of its accompaniment) so blank, barren, unintelligible as *Nature immense.* I take it that Berlioz is illustrating Faust's disengagement from the natural world to which he struggles to unite himself: he can only clumsily, haltingly, join his voice to the wind, the torrent, the avalanche.[23]

The last we hear from Faust comes during the Ride into the Abyss. Around the year 1800 Goethe wrote a plan for his future sketches of *Faust* that included an "Epilogue in Chaos on the way to Hell."[24] Berlioz could not have known that, but the existence of this plan shows again Berlioz's astonishing sensitivity to the submerged aspects of Goethe's *Faust*—it is again as if Berlioz realized a Faust that Goethe decided to suppress, a kind of negative inversion, passive and querulous, of the active, extravagant, onward-striving Faust that Goethe cherished. The Ride to the Abyss is one of the most startling passages in all of Romantic music: it begins with a fast gallop in the strings, on top of which there rides a peculiar oboe tune (example 21). (This effect is not quite unprecedented in Berlioz's canon: the ending of *Herminie* is written to a similar plan.) The oboe tune consists mostly of triads, altering key to match the galloping strings, from C minor to D♭ major and other keys; I cannot explain why the oboe gives the impression of being eerily unrelated to the galloping, unless this effect is due to the difference in speed. What does this mean? I argue that, in a work in which Faust's irrelevance and abstraction are so strongly described, that the oboe represents Faust's failure to engage himself even with the horror of his own damnation: he remains aloof, almost schizophrenically remote, an oboe whistling in the dark, while the strings rush him to hell.[25] Part of Faust screams out in shock at the rain of blood, the thunder rumbling underground; but part of Faust remains inviolate, immune, critical, on a private plane of musical discourse, on a private planet. This scene is perhaps the greatest triumph of the rhetoric of psychological disjunction that Berlioz developed in the *Symphonie fantastique* and *Harold en Italie.*

Example 21. Faust whistles in the dark

The musical representation of Pandemonium is as impressive as that of the Ride to the Abyss. What happens to Faust as he enters hell? The text refers vaguely to *un mystère d'horreur*; but our hopes of understanding just what horrible mystery is taking place are thwarted by the fact that the devils who welcome Faust sing in gibberish. Berlioz was attracted to meaningless languages: he wrote a nonsense text for a chorus (based on some music from *La mort de Cléopâtre*), and was delighted that it frustrated the Papal censors;[26] and the Nubian slave girls entertain Queen Dido in the fourth act of *Les Troyens* (1858) by dancing to some cries in their (imaginary) native language. In *La damnation de Faust,* this loss of meaning is the final extension of the urge toward randomness, incoherence of being, that has been a feature of Faust's quest from the beginning—an urge toward nonentity. In one sense, Faust is so null, so pre-damned before he ever meets Méphistophélès, that he only seeks to make explicit the vacuum that constitutes him: he seeks to embody himself in ever more impressive structures of meaninglessness. Faust has been experimenting with various musical and dramatic contexts, with various identities—Christian rejoicer, tavern-carouser, suave seducer—but all these contexts, these identities, though right for many people, are wrong for Faust. By descending to hell he only finds a more aggressive, forthright absence of meaning; but he was equally insignificant, irrelevant, on the plains of Hungary or in Marguerite's room.

The musical structure of Pandemonium precisely matches the verbal structure of nonsense syllables: a chaos of juxtaposed poorly related, (mostly) major triads, initially moving from B major to F major, then to F♯ major;

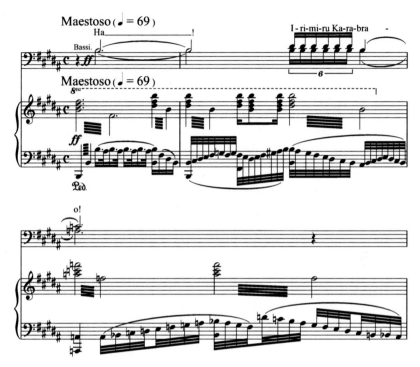

Example 22. Pandemonium

the clash of chords separated by a minor second, such as B major and C major or F major and F♯ major, or of chords separated by a tritone, such as B major and F major, is Berlioz's method for representing the perfect inconsequence of hell (example 22).[27] Pandemonium is an extension of Méphistophélès' motto, the musical quotation mark that often signals his presence: three fast brassy major chords, in consecutive staccato sixteenth-notes, falling by semitones (such as D♭–C–B)—a figure probably derived from the accompaniment of Méphistophélès' song of the flea. Berlioz lavished major triads on his demons probably in order to make the non-functionality (or purely semantic functionality) of the harmonic progressions all the more apparent.

Still, one wonders what exactly is happening to the damned Faust on the mental stage of the dramatic legend. There are clues from several sources. In the original chapbook of 1587, Faust allows demons, at the end of his contracted period with Mephistopheles, to tear apart his living body in the hope that he can thereby avoid the damnation of his soul. And, as it happens, Berlioz was particularly fascinated by the idea of dismemberment or mutilation. In his Prix de Rome cantata *La mort d'Orphée* (1827), Berlioz wrote a graphic musical description of Orpheus torn asunder by the Bacchants; in the first act of *Les Troyens,* Énée makes his sudden entrance to describe exactly how (with abrupt sinuous low brass) the serpents squeezed the life out of Laocoön (Schumann noted presciently, in 1835, that "Music is to Berlioz like the snake to Laocoön"[28]); in the *Requiem* (1837), Berlioz wrote an astonishing Lacrymosa movement in a spastic 9/8 rhythm, which sounds like an infernal machine for tearing apart the damned, limb from limb; and in the *Te Deum* (1855), Berlioz wrote a *Judex crederis* movement, another sort of apocalyptic device, this time for pounding the damned souls flat. I suspect that Faust's fate can be imagined along similar lines: as he enters Pandemonium, the harmonic clashes rend him in pieces.

5. The Dismemberment of Berlioz

Goethe referred to his *Faust* as a sponge colony—a perfect metaphor for a sort of indeterminate organic form that can effortlessly disperse itself, re-unite itself, transform itself, without losing its integrity, its tenacity of be-ing. Goethe's *Faust* is a set of strange, unstageably mobile scenes, often without any strong temporal sequence, slowly accreted over a lifetime— the poem itself is a huge sponge. Similarly Berlioz's whole canon is a kind of sponge: the separate pieces are extremely diverse, and yet they seem to move together into some loose enormous integrity, to investigate possibili-ties for some single purpose. As Yeats once wrote, "There is for every man some one scene, some one adventure, some one picture that is the image of his secret life"[29]—what is Berlioz's one scene, one adventure? I think one might understand Berlioz's canon as a set of works cooperant to-ward one story, a story about positive and negative genius. *La mort d'Orphée,* the *Symphonie fantastique, La damnation de Faust* all tell one side of the story, the myth of catastrophe: how genius verges on such extremes of inspiration that it tears itself apart, undergoes a kind of ritual sacrifice. There is biographical evidence to support the notion that Berlioz identified himself with this sort of negative genius—as he wrote in an impassioned letter (1830) about his disappointed love for Harriet Smithson:

> Will she understand the poetry of my love? . . . Oh! Juliet, Ophelia, Belvidera [from Otway's *Venice Preserv'd*], Jeanne Shore [from Rowe's *Jane Shore*—all these are roles played by Harriet], names that hell cease-lessly repeats. . . .
> I am a very unfortunate man, a being almost isolated in the world, an animal crushed by an imagination that it cannot support, devoured by a limitless love that is repaid only with indifference and scorn. . . . Oh! sublime ones! exterminate me![30]

This is of course the emotional situation behind the *Symphonie fantastique,* in which Miss Smithson is represented by the *idée fixe,* and the prayer for annihilation is realized during the scaffold scene. The phrase "an animal crushed by an imagination that it cannot support" is also suggestive of *La damnation de Faust,* where Faust's imagination seems to lie entirely outside his own mind, in the insupportable figure of Méphistophélès—Faust is a kind of anti-genius persecuted by images devised by some alien, hostile intelligence.

But for every dismemberment there is a resurrection. In *La mort d'Orphée,* Orpheus' lyre seems to live on, plinking beautiful music without any human agent, after the poet is torn asunder. The hero of the *Symphonie fantastique,* executed in the fourth movement and sent to hell in the fifth, returns to life, impassioned, artistically gifted, even orgiastic, in *Lélio* (1832), Berlioz's peculiar parergon to his symphony. (*Lélio* is arguably an apprentice semi-opera: throughout *Lélio* integuments of speech keep growing forth, to hold together the scattered musical pieces.) The affiliation between *La mort d'Orphée* and *Lélio* is strong: in fact Berlioz stole the postlude from Orpheus and inserted it into *Lélio* as *La harpe éolienne*—as if the lyre's resurrection could assist in the resurrection of any genius. If *La damnation de Faust* has a positive counterpart, it is *Benvenuto Cellini* (1838), Berlioz's fullest study of positive genius, genius like a volcano or fireworks exploding in the head, inspiration like electricity applied to the scalp, as in the famous wild-haired caricatures of Berlioz himself. Cellini has several features in common with Lélio: Lélio is attracted to thieves, Cellini kills a man with his sword; Lélio measures himself against Goethe and Shakespeare, Cellini measures himself against Michelangelo. The opera even hints at a rhythm of dismemberment and resurrection: in the fifth scene of the first act, the villain Fieramosca compares himself to Orpheus torn apart by the Bacchantes. Cellini's great opponent is inertia: the inertia of social tradition (which refuses to allow the daughter of a treasurer to marry a Florentine rogue), the inertia of artistic tradition (which demands an art of conventional, unthreatening character), the inertia of money (which rewards mediocre proficiency, not aesthetic excellence), the sheer inertia of stone or metal itself, against which a sculptor labors to realize the fluid visionary forms in his mind. The opera offers many musical symbols for inertia, notably the vulgar ophicleide tune that depicts the feigned Balducci singing before the Papal moneybags (1.13); the implacable and invariant chant of the Innkeeper, demanding payment for his bill (1.9); and the slack enervating folksong-like melody *Bienheureux les matelots* by which the laborers on the Perseus statue dampen their own spirits, render themselves unable to assist creation (2.9). Similarly Berlioz provides musical counter-symbols for the fire that melts the bronze, for the hammer, for Cellini's shaping force, spurting vigor. In Berlioz's canon, the artistic imagination has extreme power, either to energize the mind or to destroy it; in this way Cellini and Faust are the two halves of one genius.

Dismemberment	Resurrection
La mort d'Orphée	Postlude to *La mort d'Orphée*
Symphonie fantastique	*Lélio*
La damnation de Faust	*Benvenuto Cellini*

6. Toward Gounod

Perhaps it would be appropriate to end with a glance at the musical future of Goethe's Faust. Of course, his chief refuge was to be the old-folks' home of the much-admired, much-despised opera of Gounod. We've seen how radically Berlioz reorganized, recomposed the character of Faust. Berlioz's Faust is a Byronic figure who keeps commenting on how bored he is—the word *ennui* is rarely far from his lips; and, like Byron's Manfred (1.1.144), his profoundest desire is for self-oblivion. But Gounod's Faust is in many ways a genuinely Goethean figure. Indeed precisely those parts of the opera that are often deplored—the cheapness of Méphistophélès' illusions, the meretriciousness of Marguerite dazzled by the jewels—are the parts of the opera that best extrapolate Goethe's vision. Goethe's poem is highly artificial, histrionic, "operatic" in the vexing sense of the term—it is a poem about a brilliant thinker trapped in contentless structures of thought. Even Gretchen, though she in some sense "stands" for humble authenticity of feeling, is largely a conventional figure from eighteenth-century melodrama. To write an opera in which Faust is continually teased by the closed forms of beautiful melodies, disconnected, absurdly profuse, seems to me a splendid way of realizing the predicament of Goethe's character. I yield to no one in my admiration of Boïto's *Mefistofele* (1868), or Busoni's posthumous *Doktor Faustus* (1925), or Schnittke's *Historia von D. Johann Fausten* (1995—both Busoni and Schnittke stray far from Goethe), or, of course, Berlioz's *La damnation de Faust*; but it seems to me quite correct that the first Faust-opera that comes into the public mind is Gounod's. Only Gounod was sufficiently sensitive to the sublime silliness of Goethe's poem, its *hoher Leichtsinn*. If Goethe's *Faust* is a tragedy attempting to become an opera, as Goethe himself described it,[31] the opera it is working toward is that written by Gounod, no other. But the tragedy—*that* Berlioz found, and found with unique success.

Notes

Preface

1. See Fernand Baldensperger's *avant-propos* to Nerval's *Les deux Faust de Goethe*, pp. vi–vii.

Chapter 1

1. See *The Critical Tradition*, ed. Richter, p. 231.
2. See Mervyn James, *English Politics and the Concept of Honour*, p. 15.
3. See ibid., pp. 5–6.
4. See René Girard, *A Theater of Envy*, p. 17.
5. This, and all subsequent quotations from Shakespeare, are taken from *The Riverside Shakespeare*.
6. See *The Critical Tradition*, ed. Richter, p. 235.
7. See Samuel Taylor Coleridge, *Biographia Literaria*, pp. 304–5.
8. See Baldesar Castiglione, *The Book of the Courtier*, p. 68.
9. This translation is based on the Italian text of Petrocchi and Singleton.
10. See Coleridge, *Lectures upon Shakespeare and Other Dramatists*.
11. See *The Critical Tradition*, ed. Richter, p. 235.

Chapter 2

1. See Norman Rabkin, *Shakespeare and the Problem of Meaning*, pp. 81–82.
2. See ibid., p. 117.
3. David Garrick, *The Plays of David Garrick*, vol. 3: *Garrick's Adaptations of Shakespeare, 1744–1756*, pp. 143–44.
4. See *Four Centuries of Shakespearean Criticism*, ed. Kermode, p. 73 (translator uncredited).
5. Translated from Victor Hugo, *La préface de Cromwell*, ed. Souriau, pp. 22–23.
6. Translated from Berlioz, *Memoires* 1, pp. 215–16.
7. Ibid. 1, p. 125.
8. Ibid. 1, pp. 127–28.

Chapter 3

1. Berlioz, *Memoires* 1, pp. 221–22. It is remarkable how Berlioz manages to create musical effects in his prose, such as this crescendo / diminuendo achieved through careful calibration of the number of exclamation points.
2. Ibid. 1, pp. 229–30.
3. Ibid. 1, pp. 269–70.

4. Ibid. 1, pp. 274–75.

5. See, for example, John Warrack, in *The Wagner Companion,* ed. Burbidge and Sutton, p. 112.

6. *Mémoires* 2, p. 196.

7. Ibid. 1, pp. 163–64.

8. Ibid. 1, p. 278.

9. Translated from Berlioz, *À travers chants,* pp. 151–52.

10. Ibid., p. 160. The original of Rousseau's essay, *Fragments d'observations sur "L'Alceste" italien de M. le Chevalier Gluck,* may be found in Jean-Jacques Rousseau, *Oeuvres complètes,* édition publiée sous la direction de Bernard Gagnebin et Marcel Raymond, 5 vols., Bibliothèque de la Pléiade (Paris: Gallimard, 1959–95), 5:441–57.

11. Ibid., p. 323.

12. Ibid., p. 325.

13. *Mémoires* 1, p. 291.

14. Ibid. 2, p. 237.

15. From the Kalmus vocal score, K 06090.

16. See Julian Rushton, *Berlioz: Roméo et Juliette,* p. 24.

17. I thank David Gramit for suggesting this line of speculation.

18. *Mémoires* 2, p. 32.

19. See Levy's "'Ritter Berlioz' in Germany," in *Berlioz Studies,* ed. Bloom, p. 144.

20. *À travers chants,* p. 29.

21. Ibid., p. 31.

22. Ibid., p. 44.

23. The following outline is based on that in the Bärenreiter edition of the vocal score of *Roméo et Juliette,* BA 5458a, piano reduction by Eike Wernhard (Kassel: Bärenreiter, 1995).

24. For a brilliant—indeed Berliozian—reading of the irony in the *O Freunde* section of the Ninth Symphony, see Stephen Hinton's "Not *Which* Tones? The Crux of Beethoven's Ninth," *19th-Century Music* 22/1 (Summer 1998), pp. 61–77.

25. *Mémoires* 2, p. 35.

26. Jacques Chailley, "Roméo et Juliette," *Revue de Musicologie* 63 (1977): 117.

27. *Mémoires* 2, pp. 307, 375.

28. I owe this explanation of the function of the *idée fixe* to Su Yin Mak.

29. Translated by Rushton, in his *Berlioz: Roméo et Juliette,* p. 90.

30. *Mémoires* 1, pp. 219–20. I wonder whether Berlioz knew Biber's *Battalia a 10,* which generates a remarkable cacophony, as the instrumentalists impersonate drunken soldiers, each playing a patriotic tune from a different land, all at the same time—a late seventeenth-century anticipation of Charles Ives. Jennifer Brown notes that something like the *English concert* of Berlioz persists in modern English pantomimes, in which a group of children is divided in two: each semichorus sings a different song, as loudly as possible.

31. *Mémoires* 2, p. 36.

32. Berlioz, *Correspondance générale* #1135 (to Dominique Tajan-Rogé, London, 10 November 1847)—in this letter Berlioz writes out the love theme in musical notation, so that his correspondent can savor it too.

33. See Holoman, *Berlioz,* p. 265.

34. See Rushton, *Berlioz: Roméo et Juliette,* p. 107.

35. *À travers chants,* pp. 519–20.

36. Ibid., p. 36.

37. Translated from Berlioz, *Les soirées de l'orchestre,* pp. 317–18.

38. Translated by Rushton, in his *Berlioz: Roméo et Juliette,* p. 90.

39. Rushton makes these identifications in ibid., pp. 37–38, and it is not easy to imagine a formalist severe enough to dispute them.

40. There is a curious sequel, in that Brahms evidently borrowed this passage in the first movement of his Double Concerto (1887), where it sounds like a gloomy memory of extinct triumph.

41. See Rushton, *Berlioz: Roméo et Juliette,* p. 41.

42. *Mémoires* 1, p. 224.

43. The new time signature looks like half the previous one, but the metronome mark requires each beat of 3/4 to equal the previous measure of 3/8, so that the triplet eighths come out the same as the eighths in 3/8. I owe this explanation to Julian Rushton.

44. *Mémoires* 1, p. 121. The clown was Nahum Tate.

45. Bärenreiter score, p. 104.

46. See Roland Barthes, *The Responsibility of Forms,* p. 299. This is a translation of his 1982 book, *L'Obvie et l'obtus.*

47. *Mémoires* 1, p. 63.

48. *Correspondance générale* #1108 (to Franz Liszt, St. Petersburg, 27 April/9 May [1847]).

49. Chailley, "*Roméo et Juliette,*" p. 118.

50. *À travers chants,* p. 55.

Chapter 4

1. See Jane K. Brown, *Goethe's Faust,* p. 75.

2. See Heinrich Wölfflin, *The Sense of Form in Art,* pp. 31, 44, 46. This is a translation of *Italien und das deutsche Formgefühl* (1931).

3. Wölfflin, *The Sense of Form in Art,* p. 59.

4. Citations from Marlowe's *Dr. Faustus* are from Roma Gill's edition.

5. Joseph Conrad, *Heart of Darkness,* p. 61.

6. W. H. Auden, *Collected Poems,* p. 338.

7. The German text that is the basis for this, and all subsequent translations from Part One of *Faust,* is from *Goethe's Faust,* ed. R.-M. S. Heffner. The German text I used for Part Two is from *Faust: Der Tragödie zweiter Teil.*

8. Coleridge, *Biographia Literaria,* p. 304.

9. Note that John Warrack has similarly described Berlioz as the fabricator of mental theatres: see "Berlioz and the Theatre of the Mind," reprinted in Aprahamian's *Essays on Music,* pp. 49–52.

10. See Keith Pollard's essay in the recording of Schumann's *Scenes from Goethe's Faust,* London LP 12100. Also note Goethe's statement in *Naturphilosophie:* "No living thing is unitary in nature: every such thing is a plurality. Even the organism which appears to us as individual exists as a collection of independent living entities. . . . In part these entities are joined from the outset, in part they find their way

together to form a union. They diverge and then seek each other again; everywhere and in every way they thus work to produce a chain of creation without end" (Goethe, *Scientific Studies,* p. 307).

11. See Kafka's short story, "Beim Bau der Chinesischen Mauer."

12. See section 7 of Nietzsche's *Der Fall Wagner.*

13. See Jane K. Brown, *Goethe's Faust,* p. 104.

14. See Auden, *Collected Poems,* p. 522.

15. See W. H. Auden, *The Dyer's Hand,* p. 328.

16. See John Fuegi, *Brecht & Co.,* p. 77.

17. For example, see *A Midsummer Night's Dream* 2.1.50.

18. See Pater, *The Renaissance* (1893), p. 181.

19. Ibid., pp. 51–52.

20. Ibid., p. 50.

21. Ibid., p. 171.

22. Ibid., p. 185.

23. See Goethe, *Conversations with Eckermann,* 20 Dec. 1829.

24. Ibid., 17 Feb. 1831.

25. Ibid., 21 Feb. 1831.

26. See William Blake, *The Complete Poetry & Prose of William Blake,* p. 36.

27. Goethe, *Conversations with Eckermann,* 18 Apr. 1827.

Chapter 5

1. There has long been some doubt whether the translation was entirely Nerval's own work, since Nerval's German was not excellent—the poet Heine in fact advised Nerval to find a German woman and marry her, simply to improve his linguistic skills. See Fernand Baldensperger's *avant-propos* in Nerval, *Les deux Faust de Goethe,* pp. iv, ix.

2. Goethe, *Conversations with Eckermann,* 3 Jan. 1830.

3. See Holoman, *Berlioz,* p. 53.

Chapter 6

1. See Auden, *The Dyer's Hand,* p. 119.

2. See Griffiths' notes to Oiseau-Lyre CD 425 943–2, p. 20.

3. *Mémoires* 1, p. 123.

4. See Reeve, "*The Damnation of Faust,* or the Perils of Heroism in Music," in *Berlioz Studies,* ed. Bloom, chap. 17, p. 65.

5. See Hermann Hofer, "Faust einmal ganz anders: 'La damnation de Faust' von Hector Berlioz neu gelesen," *Lendemains* 31 (1983): 35.

6. See Thomas Mann, *Doktor Faustus,* chap. 45, p. 477.

7. See George Gordon, Lord Byron, *Byron: The Oxford Authors,* pp. 125–26.

8. *Mémoires* 1, p. 298.

9. Julian Rushton notes that the tunes that Berlioz ascribed to Faust share certain salient features: a collection of Faust quotations "shows no fewer than seven-

teen shapes falling from $\hat{5}$ to $\hat{3}$ or $\hat{2}$. All come at significant points in the role. . . . But the quest for precise meaning to these shapes is fraught with danger. The most important [the $\hat{5}$ to $\hat{3}$ or $\hat{2}$ shape] is neither positive nor negative, but a structural link. . . . Another element associated with Faust is a pronounced chromaticism"; as for key structure, Faust adheres "to F♯ minor, [even] in those piece not in that key . . . His excursion to its pun, F♮, in his air, might symbolize his entry into Margaret's domain, even the heavenly domain; it is the key of 'Chant de la fête de Pâques' . . . and Margaret's two songs" (*The Musical Language of Berlioz,* pp. 231, 253–54).

   10. *Mémoires* 1, pp. 54–55.
   11. See David Cairns, *Berlioz,* vol. 1, *The Making of an Artist,* p. 367.
   12. See Robert Schumann, *Schumann on Music,* p. 79.
   13. Ibid., p. 83.
   14. Ibid., p. 83.
   15. Ibid., p. 78.
   16. See Arnold Schoenberg, *Style and Idea,* pp. 394–95: "the Royal Theme . . . did not admit one single canonic imitation."
   17. Gustav Mahler, toward the end of the Romantic movement, was quite fond of rising scalar nature-themes, as *Lob des hohen Verstandes* and the third song in *Das Lied von der Erde* demonstrate.
   18. *Mémoires* 2, p. 247.
   19. This outline of *La damnation de Faust* is based on the one given in the New Berlioz Edition of the work, vol. 18.
   20. See Berlioz, *Les grotesques de la musique,* pp. 31–32.
   21. The naked scale to which Berlioz set, in his *Requiem* (1837), the words *Rex tremendae majestatis* (King of fearful majesty) gives something of the quality of terror to be found in the scalar figures of *Nature immense,* though the *Rex tremendae* scale isn't dotted.
   22. Cited in "The Paris Operas of Gluck," by Jeremy Hayes, from EMI LP SLS 1077513, p. 7.
   23. Julian Rushton hears this passage similarly: "Even in this last utterance Faust (for all his protestations) is out of tune with his surroundings, the wild natural counterpart to the rural peace of Part I. . . . The orchestration is pretty consistently anti-functional. The brass appears to underline cadential goals but adds little to the most important of all" (*The Musical Language of Berlioz,* pp. 231, 248). Musically speaking, nature goes one way, Faust another.
   24. See Goethe, *Faust: A Tragedy* (Norton Critical Edition) p. 396.
   25. Another view might identify the oboe with Marguerite, by analogy with the female oboe-impersonations in *Le roi Lear* and *Roméo et Juliette.*
   26. *Mémoires* 1, p. 283—this shadow-chorus now appears in *Lélio,* with ordinary French words.
   27. Compare Rushton: "At times Berlioz seems to be using tritone relations for devilishness. This is most conspicuous in the huge B and F chords of 'Pandaemonium' (*The Musical Language of Berlioz,* p. 254).
   28. *Schumann on Music,* p. 79.
   29. See W. B. Yeats, *Essays and Introductions,* p. 95.
   30. *Correspondance générale* #156 (to Ferdinand Hiller, 3 March 1830).
   31. Goethe, *Conversations with Eckermann,* 25 Jan. 1827.

Bibliography of Works Cited in the Text

Aprahamian, Felix, ed. *Essays on Music: An Anthology from "The Listener."* London: Cassell, 1967.

Auden, W. H. *Collected Poems.* Edited by Edward Mendelson. New York: Random House, 1976.

————. *The Dyer's Hand and Other Essays.* New York: Random House, 1962.

Barthes, Roland. *The Responsibility of Forms: Critical Essays on Music, Arts, and Representation.* Translated by Richard Howard. New York: Hill and Wang, 1985.

Berlioz, Hector. *À travers chants: Études musicales, adorations, boutades et critiques.* Paris: Michel Lévy, 1862.

————. *Correspondance générale.* Edited under the direction of Pierre Citron. Paris: Flammarion, 1972 (vol. 1, 1803–1832) and 1978 (vol. 3, 1842–1850).

————. *Les grotesques de la musique.* Paris: Librairie Nouvelle, 1859.

————. *Mémoires.* Chronology and introduction by Pierre Citron. 2 vols. Paris: Garnier-Flammarion, 1969.

————. *Les soirées de l'orchestre.* Paris: Michel Lévy, 1854.

Blake, William. *The Complete Poetry & Prose of William Blake.* Newly revised edition, edited by David V. Erdman, with commentary by Harold Bloom. Garden City, N.Y.: Anchor Books, 1982.

Bloom, Peter, ed. *Berlioz Studies.* Cambridge: Cambridge University Press, 1992.

Brooke, Arthur. *Brooke's 'Romeus and Juliet,' Being the Original of Shakespeare's 'Romeo and Juliet.'* New York: Duffield, 1908.

Brown, Jane K. *Goethe's Faust: The German Tragedy.* Ithaca, N.Y.: Cornell University Press, 1986.

Burbidge, Peter, and Richard Sutton, eds.. *The Wagner Companion.* London: Faber and Faber, 1979.Byron, George Gordon, Lord. *Byron: The Oxford Authors.* Edited by Jerome J. McGann. Oxford: Oxford University Press, 1986.

Cairns, David. *Berlioz.* Vol. 1, *The Making of an Artist.* Berkeley: University of California Press, 2000.

Castiglione, Baldesar. *The Book of the Courtier.* Translated by George Bull. London: Penguin Books, 1976.

Chailley, Jacques, "*Roméo et Juliette.*" *Revue de Musicologie* 63 (1977): 115–22.

Coleridge, Samuel Taylor. *Biographia Literaria.* Edited by James Engell and W. Jackson Bate. Princeton, N.J.: Princeton University Press, 1983.

————. *Lectures upon Shakespeare and Other Dramatists.* New York: Harper and Brothers, 1884.

Conrad, Joseph. *Heart of Darkness.* Edited by Robert Kimbrough. New York: W. W. Norton, 1971.

Dante Alighieri. *The Divine Comedy.* Edited by Giorgio Petrocchi and Charles Singleton. Princeton, N.J.: Princeton University Press, 1977.

Fuegi, John. *Brecht and Company: Sex, Politics, and the Making of the Modern Drama.* New York: Grove Press, 1994.

Garrick, David. *The Plays of David Garrick.* Vol. 3: *Garrick's Adaptations of Shakespeare, 1744–1756.* Edited by Harry William Pedicord and Frederick Louis Bergman. Carbondale: Southern Illinois University Press, 1981.

Girard, René. *A Theater of Envy / William Shakespeare.* New York: Oxford University Press, 1991.

Goethe, J. W. *Conversations with Eckermann (1823–1832).* Translated by John Oxenford. San Francisco, Calif.: North Point Press, 1984.

———. *Faust: A Tragedy.* Translated by Walter Arndt. Edited by Cyrus Hamlin. New York: W. W. Norton, 1976.

———. *Faust: Der Tragödie zweiter Teil.* Stuttgart: Philipp Reclam Jun., 1986.

———. *Goethe's Faust.* Edited by R.-M. S. Heffner et al. Boston: D. C. Heath, 1954.

———. *Scientific Studies.* Edited and translated by Donald Miller. New York: Suhrkamp, 1988.

Hinton, Stephen. "Not *Which* Tones? The Crux of Beethoven's Ninth." *19th-Century Music* 22/1 (Summer 1998): 61–77.

Hofer, Hermann. "Faust einmal ganz anders: 'La damnation de Faust' von Hector Berlioz neu gelesen." *Lendemains* 31 (1983): 35.

Holoman, D. Kern. *Berlioz.* Cambridge, Mass.: Harvard University Press, 1989.

Hugo, Victor. *La Préface de Cromwell: Introduction, texte, et notes.* Edited by Maurice Souriau. Paris: Boivin, 193–?.

James, Mervyn. *English Politics and the Concept of Honour 1485–1642.* Oxford: Past and Present Society, 1978.

Kermode, Frank, ed. *Four Centuries of Shakespearian Criticism.* New York: Avon Library, 1965.

Mann, Thomas: *Doktor Faustus.* Frankfurt: Taschenbuch Verlag, 1973.

Marlowe, Christopher. *Doctor Faustus.* Edited by Roma Gill. New York: Hill and Wang, 1966.

Nerval, Gérard de. *Les deux Faust de Goethe.* Edited by Fernand Baldensperger. Paris: Librairie ancienne Honoré Champion, 1932.

Nietzsche, Friedrich. *Der Fall Wagner: Ein Musikanten-Problem.* Leipzig: C. G. Naumann, 1888.

Pater, Walter. *The Renaissance* (1893). Edited by Donald L. Hill. Berkeley: University of California Press, 1980.

Rabkin, Norman. *Shakespeare and the Problem of Meaning.* Chicago: University of Chicago Press, 1981.

Richter, David H., ed. *The Critical Tradition: Classic Texts and Contemporary Trends.* New York: St. Martin's Press, 1989.

Rousseau, Jean-Jacques. *Fragments d'observations sur "L'Alceste" de M. le Chevalier de Gluck* (1778). In his *Oeuvres complètes,* édition publiée sous la direction de Bernard Gagnebin et Marcel Raymond, 5:441–57. 5 vols. Bibliothèque de la Pléiade. Paris: Gallimard, 1959–1995.

Rushton, Julian. *Berlioz: Roméo et Juliette.* Cambridge: Cambridge University Press, 1994.

———. *The Musical Language of Berlioz.* Cambridge: Cambridge University Press, 1983.

Schoenberg, Arnold. *Style and Idea: Selected Writings of Arnold Schoenberg.* Edited by Leonard Stein. Translated by Leo Black. London: Faber and Faber, 1975.

Schumann, Robert. *Schumann on Music: A Selection from the Writings.* Translated and edited by Henry Pleasants. New York: Dover, 1965.

Shakespeare, William. *The Riverside Shakespeare.* Edited by G. Blakemore Evans et al. Boston: Houghton Mifflin, 1974.

Wölfflin, Heinrich. *The Sense of Form in Art: A Comparative Psychological Study.* Translated by Alice Muehsam and Norma Shatan. New York: Chelsea, 1958.

Yeats, W. B. *Essays and Introductions.* New York: Macmillan, 1961.

Index

Berlioz's Semi-Operas studies two works, *Roméo et Juliette* and *La damnation de Faust*, which are among the most challenging of the entire Romantic movement, not least because they assault the notion of genre: they take place in a sort of limbo between symphony and opera, and try to fulfill the highest goals of each *simultaneously*. Berlioz strenuously resisted any impediments that stood in the way of complete compositional freedom. Most of his large-scale works nevertheless obey the strictures of some preexistent form, whether opera or symphony or mass or cantata; it is chiefly in these two experiments that Berlioz allowed himself full liberty to be Berlioz.

One of the central characteristics of Romanticism is the belief that all arts are one, that literature, painting, and music have a common origin and a common goal; and this book shows what Berlioz did to achieve a *Gesamtkunstwerk,* a fusion of arts, in a manner even more impressive (in certain respects) than that of Wagner, in that Berlioz implicated into his total-art-work texts by two of the greatest poets of Western literature, Shakespeare and Goethe.

The method of this book is unusual in that it pays equally close attention to the original literary texts (*Romeo and Juliet* and *Faust*) as well as to the musical adaptations; furthermore, it suggests many analogues in the operatic world that Berlioz knew—the world of Gluck, Mozart, Mehul, Spontini, Cherubini—in order to show exactly how Berlioz followed or flouted the dramatic conventions of his age.

Berlioz's Semi-Operas contributes to Berlioz studies, to studies of the Romantic movement, and to the rapidly growing field of comparative arts.

Daniel Albright is Richard L. Turner Professor in the Humanities at the University of Rochester.